BROKEN SNARE

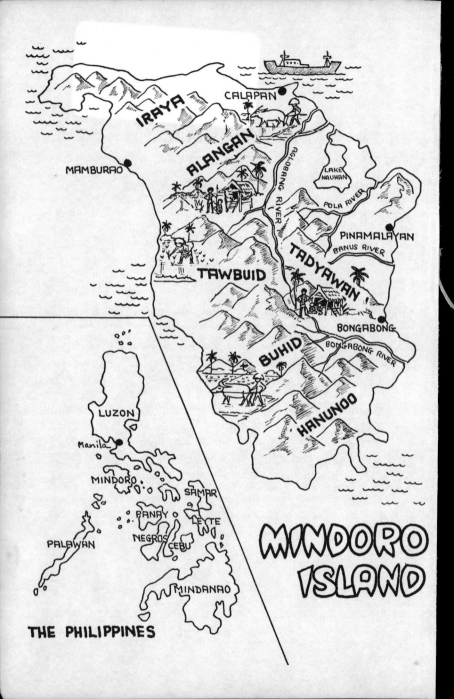

Broken Snare

by

CAROLINE STICKLEY

"We have escaped as a bird
from the snare of the fowlers;
the snare is broken,
and we have escaped!"

Psalm 124.7 RSV

OMF BOOKS

© OVERSEAS MISSIONARY FELLOWSHIP

First published in the United Kingdom   *January 1975*
Reprinted   . .   . .   *October 1975*
Reprinted   . .   . .   *April 1979*

Acknowledgement

I am grateful to Fay Goddard, who formerly
worked in a neighbouring tribe. Her optimism has
kept me writing and her advice has been
invaluable.   C.S.

ISBN 0 85363 102 6

Made in Great Britain

*Published by the Overseas Missionary Fellowship
Belmont, The Vine, SEVENOAKS, Kent, TN13 3TZ
and printed and bound at The Camelot Press Ltd, Southampton*

Contents

Foreword

Caroline Stickley was one of a group of single girls of the Overseas Missionary Fellowship tribal team who gave the best part of their lives to take the gospel to neglected Philippine tribes. As their superintendent, I was in a position to observe at first hand the unique adventure she describes. She carries her readers into the forests of the island of Mindoro and into the incredibly primitive lives of its tribal people in such a way that we feel like invisible witnesses of their intimate day-to-day existence. She has lived so close to these people for so long that she seems unaware of just how remarkable her story is. She tells it with an amazing nonchalance and without an ounce of self-pity.

The vast archipelago of south-east Asian islands shelters an immense variety of primitive peoples, often living within easy reach of highly sophisticated and ancient cultures. Among these are the tribespeople of Mindoro. Less than two hundred miles from Manila, the capital of the Philippines, they live a thousand years behind their fellow-countrymen in development. Unlike the savagely colourful stone-age tribes of New Guinea, with their paint and feathers, dances and warfare, Mindoro's tribesmen are simple, peaceful forest-dwellers, clinging to life through an expert knowledge of jungle-lore. Near-starvation, disease and merciless exploitation by unscrupulous men in the lowlands have kept them dependent upon a precarious semi-migratory way of life with slash-and-burn, dibble-stick "agriculture" to supplement the wild foods gathered from the jungle. But dominating their lives are the evil spirits and the men who wield power as mediums and sorcerers. No people are more enslaved, caught and held like birds, in the devil's snare. And no more appropriate title for this book could be found than one which represents them as being delivered from that snare to enjoy their freedom within the family of God.

Broken Snare is primarily about the Tadyawan tribe, but in many ways the story is typical of the battle to free the captives in all six of Mindoro's tribes. When the first contacts were made with these people, more than twenty years ago, the rigorous nature of the life ahead for missionary pioneers became apparent—the long, hot treks with pack on back, the fording of strong mountain rivers, the stumbling along uneven forest trails, the climbing of steep hillsides and the encountering of known and unknown hazards, rope bridges, wild animals, snakes and leeches innumerable. Two methods of approach were open. Either the pioneers could retain as many Western safeguards and comforts as possible, to offset the inevitable hardships, or they could start by living as much like the tribespeople as possible, gradually adding whatever they needed to preserve their health and efficiency. For Jesus' sake they chose the second option— and to this day, more than two decades later, they live for weeks on end with an austerity that could hardly be increased without serious detriment to their health. Small wonder, then, that Caroline Stickley can write so intimately of the Tadyawan and neighbouring Tawbuid, and so graphically of the struggle that led to the escape of many from the devil's clutches, like birds from the fowler's snare.

A. J. Broomhall

1 The Snare Holds

March, 1957. The dry season on Mindoro Island of the Philippines was at its height—hot but beautifully clear. Under my feet the earth was hard and dry, and I could hear the slap, slap of my rubber-soled "sneakers" against it as I hurried along the forest trail. I *had* to see Katubo that morning, for I was anxious to know if what I had heard the night before was true.

I emerged from the shaded path in the forest bush and squinted into the clearing where Katubo's small bark-walled house stood on its spindly legs. Katubo was sitting on the bamboo floor of his porch, splitting rattan, his brown, muscular body shiny with sweat. Judging from the stack of finished lengths beside him and from the debris scattered over the floor and on the ground under the house, this Tadyawan tribesman had been working since early morning. The sound of his knife scraping the rattan was distinct in the mid-morning quietness, interrupted only by the isolated chirp of a bird or the sawing of a cicada. I guessed his wife and children had gone off to the fields to gather sweet potatoes.

Katubo's back was toward me. When I reached him, I initiated a conversation, chatting lightly about any subject except *the* subject. Without interrupting his rhythmic splitting and scraping, and without turning to face me, Katubo answered my comments briefly, each time concluding with a nervous chuckle—a habit of his when he was uneasy. His uneasiness told me that what I had heard the previous night was true, and I knew he suspected that I had been informed.

I felt as awkward as I imagined he felt. We were friends of only a year, but good friends—he, his family and relatives, and Mary Jane and I—but now we faced the fork in the road that was going to separate us. I took a weary breath. "Katubo," I said, "is it true that neither you nor your brother's family nor your aunt's want to hear any more about Our Father in heaven?"

This time he began with his chuckle. "Yes, it's true," he said, then chuckled again and went on splitting, still with his back toward me.

"Why, Katubo?" I pursued.

"We're afraid of the demons," he answered in a lowered voice, his knife continuing to screech down the long strips of rattan.

What else could I say? I knew the background for his statement. Had they not just recently had dramatic proof in the death of his uncle Macario that the demons were angry with them? Why should they pursue their study of the Word of God and invite further catastrophe?

How I wished Katubo would at least turn around and face me, but he didn't. I knew the subject was closed, but I couldn't bring myself to walk away. It seemed impossible that this should be the abrupt end of a happy year with them.

We had moved into their little settlement on the Taghikan stream with such hope. Though only three families—seven adults and three children in all—lived on this mountain slope, they were the first Tadyawan fearless enough to welcome us into their lives. We moved in with faith, visualizing from this small start the eventual evangelization of the whole of the Tadyawan tribe.

Those early days were full of fascination. We enjoyed being with these primitive mountain people, and they showed every sign of enjoying us and our strange ways. As

the months passed, fascination deepened to friendship.
Our language knowledge increased, and our vocabulary
files fattened. The people began to understand something
of the gospel. Katubo was noticeably interested in the
message of the Book, and we had high hopes of his
becoming the first believer among the Tadyawan people.

But then came Macario's illness and the cloud it
brought over our relationship. The memories of the past
weeks took the warmth out of the sun. I could picture
again Macario lying on the floor of the hut, obviously
dying, his wife sitting beside him, sucking her pipe and
chanting to the demons while she sacrificed a chicken to
them on Macario's behalf. How we had pleaded with
both of them to trust Christ instead! And how chilling his
wife's coarse laugh as she continued her chant in defiance.

I had felt deep helplessness and defeat that day and
later again when Macario had died and the pig was
offered with raucous shouts to ward off his departed
spirit. I felt that utter helplessness all over again as I now
talked with Katubo. They were involved in the conflict of
the ages, and in the contest between the demons and the
Lord it appeared to them that the demons had won. They
felt they had no choice but to stay in favour with the
demon world.

"You may continue to live here if you want to," Katubo
added over his shoulder, "but we'll seldom be here, for
we plan to move to another mountain, only visiting our
fields here."

It was the end. We had lost our only gateway into the
Tadyawan tribe. But why had it happened? Years ago,
while still a student at Prairie Bible Institute, I had begun
praying that the Lord would prepare a people for my
coming. Hadn't the Lord heard? Hadn't He prepared
any hearts at all to receive His Word? As Mary Jane and I

packed our kerosene stove, lantern, cooking pots, clothing, and language materials and left the area, it was hard not to doubt. Six months later I left for furlough confused and questioning.

2 A Spirit Sparks Hope

What I didn't know in my defeat was that God *had* begun answering my prayer long before I first uttered it in Bible school.

When? I'm not sure. Before World War II. Perhaps just about the time I was born.

The story is a strange one. But it came to me from several sources over a period of years in long conversations around smouldering fires and under the shelter of thatched roofs. Aplaki's vision and other accounts in this book of which I was not an eyewitness are sketched as accurately as I can make them and painted with the colour of life as I came to know it.

Suddenly Aplaki stopped and stood perfectly still on the lonely forest trail, his tall naked body looking far more youthful than his grey hair suggested. Had he heard his name? He waited, ears alert. The demons maybe? He turned his head in the direction of the call. A light!—a white, dazzling light coming from the stream! Then he heard again what he thought he had heard just a moment earlier: "Aplaki, come here; let's have a chat."

Fear, confusion, and curiosity all clamoured within him for the right to govern his next move: Should he run away, or should he go and see? Tense, he took a long, deep breath. That light—it *couldn't* be demons, he reasoned, for they never appeared surrounded by such brilliance. Though fearful, he decided to investigate. He felt instinctively for his long jungle knife dangling from his waist in its wooden scabbard. Puffing on his clay pipe to drive away the gnats whirring about his sweaty body, he cautiously started off down the narrow trail that led to the stream. If it wasn't a demon, then he had nothing to fear, he assured himself.

Stepping out from the brush on to the stony bank, he involuntarily caught his breath. Standing there beside the flowing water was a beautiful spirit-being, transparent and glistening. It extended a hand to Aplaki and said, "Look in my mirror."

Aplaki, breathing deeply, approached him warily, took the mirror and looked into it, but saw nothing. The spirit pointed to a little hole in the mirror, and when Aplaki looked through the hole he could see houses and lands and islands—lots of them—the whole world probably. He was utterly baffled. What did this all mean? The spirit spoke again: "Aplaki, some day people from another land are coming to your island. They will look strange, for you have never seen anybody like them before. They will be good people, however, and they will bring good teaching. You are an old man, and you will die before they come, but you must inform your people; tell them that they should listen to those teachers and follow all that they say." With that, the spirit-being disappeared, leaving Aplaki perplexed but desperately trying to figure out the significance of what he had just witnessed.

With eyes squinting in the smoke from his pipe, he stood there meditatively toying with the three or four long grey hairs on his chin. Then, still absorbed with this awesome prophecy, he abandoned his plans to hunt for honeycombs that day and, instead, headed for home to tell the others in his large family.

His short, determined steps carried him swiftly through the greenness so familiar to his darting eyes. This forest was their forest, owned by the great-grandfathers for as far back as anybody could remember. Solid seclusion! Safety! And yet, not so safe, for while it shut them off from mean men of the outside world, it shut them in to the terrifying evils of the ancestors' spirits and the demons from the underworld who made the forest their earthly dwelling.

Aplaki knew these spirits and demons well. He had often heard their scratchings and mutterings echoing from the treetops, the rock crevices, and holes in the ground, from the cool ravines and shady streams. He had seen them, too, numberless times, housed in the bodies of men and animals, lurking in the grass outside the house or in the dark places or boldly following on the heels of his unsuspecting tribal friends. He knew that even at that moment they were awake to his every movement. He looked behind him; they were not following him! He sighed with relief at being spared the concocting of a subtle plan to give them the slip, for he was eager to get home.

He turned off on to a smaller path and minutes later stepped out of the bush into a clearing where his large palm-leaf house stood on its spindly legs, bark roof shining like copper in the mid-morning sun. From within came the voices of his sons and daughters and their families. He was glad they were still at home.

After wiping his muddy feet on one of the house legs, he strode on to the slanted stair-pole and, carelessly confident, without holding on to anything, walked up the pole, placing his calloused feet in one notch after the other until he reached the top, some six feet above the ground. He hunched his way through the covered hole of a doorway and, with body still bent, silently made his way under the low roof across the house to his own pancake-like fireplace of baked mud.

Without a word he plunked himself down heavily on the floor beside it and grabbed a sweet potato that had been left in its ashes to roast. He broke the potato in half and stuffed it into his mouth, letting the charred skin fall between the bamboo-slatted floor to the chickens and pigs below.

The rest of the folk in the house, though they knew he had returned, proceeded with preparations for leaving for their rice fields. Naked children scuffled to get the dogs tied up; some of the men were sharpening their knives on the whetstones; others stuffed tobacco leaves into their little woven pouches; the women hunted for bits of rags and tied them pirate-fashion on their heads to protect them from the scorching sun of later noon. The babies, well aware that their mothers were about to leave, screamed rebellion from the huge rattan swings where their baby-sitters held them captive, big tears streaking cleanness down their plump cheeks and dirty bare tummies.

Aplaki brushed the potato crumbs from his mouth and reached for one of the gourds hanging from the pole nearby, held it to his mouth, and gulped its cool, fresh water. He glanced all about him. He waited for the auspicious moment and, when it came, began ever so casually to mention what he had seen and heard that morning: the voice, the light, the spirit-being, the prophecy.

Commotion in the house stopped. Immediately Aplaki had the group's full attention. But questions were edged with doubt, and interest soon died in disbelief. Whoever heard of a *good* spirit visiting them? Incredible! A bit more hubbub, and the group left for the fields, leaving Aplaki very much alone.

But if his family didn't believe him, one of his mountain neighbours did.

3 Bilbino Begins His Wait

"Old One, tell me again; what did the spirit say?"

Young Bilbino's face was alive and earnest. He had to know all the details. As unusual as it was, the prophecy was something that he definitely wanted to remember. He scuttled across the floor to where Aplaki was sitting by a little lookout window in the palm-leaf wall and settled himself against a pole of the house, squirming until his bare back felt comfortable.

Aplaki removed a big safety pin from a hole in the lobe of his ear, bent over his curled-up foot, and busied himself with probing in the tough sole for an annoying thorn, at the same time uttering scattered fragments of his fascinating story.

Bilbino missed nothing of the account. Sometimes he repeated whole sentences to make sure he'd remember; sometimes he interrupted with questions, his small black eyes revealing his feelings—now fearful, now surprised, now confused, now seriously thoughtful. He believed it all. He was convinced too, like Aplaki, that the informant hadn't been a demon or an ancestor spirit.

"Old One, maybe it was your wise-one," he proposed

to Aplaki, but only half-heartedly, for in himself he didn't really feel that it could have been.

"No, Friend," corrected Aplaki, "it wasn't. I know what my wise-one looks like; he has visited me many times and has always been the same. He never looked like that wonderful one looked."

"Old One, maybe then it was a servant of one of the good spirits?"

"Yes, maybe," mused Aplaki, reaching for the hairs on his chin and twisting them slowly, first one way, then the other.

Neither talked for many minutes. Aplaki was pensive, for if what that spirit-being had said was true, he would not see those strangers when they came, for he would already be dead. Death! He hated to think about it. Even though his wise-one had promised to escort him to a good place when he died, he still shunned the thought of the actual experience of death itself. He wished he didn't have to die at all. He wished that someone would find that fountain across the seas that the great-grand-fathers had claimed gave man perpetual life. He wanted to go right on living on Mindoro's mountain slopes forever.

Bilbino's thoughts ran a different course: When would the promised strangers arrive with their good teaching? He cast a summarizing glance at Aplaki and concluded it would be a long time yet, for Aplaki was still healthy and strong, able to chop down the trees each year to make his field and set his own traps throughout the forest during the rainy season. Bilbino could only wish that somehow those teachers would soon arrive with the good teaching. So many people in their mountains needed it. Across the river some of his mountain neighbours were brutal men, beating fellow-tribesmen with sticks or with their fists at the slightest provocation or suggestion of reluctance to do what they said. He unconsciously gave his own thigh a comforting rub. It still hurt. He hoped he wouldn't meet any of them on his way home.

He stood abruptly, gave a tightening tug on his loincloth, and then announced, "I'm going now."

"All right," Aplaki replied; and Bilbino slipped through the doorway and into the forest, where every green had taken on the golden tones of the late afternoon.

As soon as Bilbino got home, he told his wife the news that some day strangers were coming with some good teaching.

"Why? Have you seen something?" she probed.

"No, but Aplaki has; a beautiful white spirit beside the stream."

"Demons," she rebutted, chuckling sarcastically.

"No, not surrounded by such brilliance as Aplaki described."

"Aplaki's wise-one then," she asserted confidently.

"No, Aplaki said it wasn't. His wise-one never looked like this one looked."

"Oh!" And she said no more.

"It might have been a servant of a good spirit," he suggested.

She grunted a don't-be-silly grunt. She was a young woman, no taller than four foot eight, a talkative, bright-eyed beauty. Bilbino was pleased that his parents had chosen her for his wife, not because she was a delight to his eye, but because she was quick, full of ambition and industry. She neither shunned work nor dawdled in it. When she was working, she didn't spare herself. Forest brush fell swiftly at the swing of her jungle knife; earth flew when she knifed through the ground for the sweet potatoes; and wicker baskets wove into being astonishingly fast under her deft fingers.

Having no name, she was merely known as Bilbino's wife. That was all that mattered to her—names weren't important; being a wife was. She was completely satisfied that her parents had fulfilled their job of finding her a suitable husband. Even the demons had given their approval of her parents' choice, for there was not one omen during the night preceding the wedding day that portended misfortune if the two were to marry—no warning voices, no prohibiting dream, no call of the koykolo bird, nothing; even the ground under the house was free of fallen ash the next morning—a very favourable sign indeed!

The signs proved true. They were happy, living in the spacious forest home of one room with the rest of Bilbino's relatives, companionably sharing in the hard work of living in a muggy jungle whose lush growth choked any aspiring thought for an easier existence. Every necessity was gained by swing of jungle knife and sweat. But they swung and they sweated, enjoying each other's fund of humour, for she was truly his equal in teasing and joking, her bright eyes always flashing, expecting his good-humoured retaliations. In the fields or at night when they came home and sank wearily on the floor near their fireplace, it was the same: chatter, teasing mockery over something that happened that day, laughter, more chatter and still more laughter. Often the friendly questioning eyes of everybody else in the household turned from their own fireplaces to the two when they heard such mirth: her laughter gusty and shrill; his, stirred from his depths, pleasantly filling the corners of the house.

The only time this atmosphere changed was when there

was some ominous threat from the demon world, forcefully reminding them—not that they ever really forgot—that theirs was a life of everlasting struggle against the power of the ever-present demons and spirits, those plotters and schemers who imprisoned a man's soul and made him sick, or devoured his soul to make him die. Their fathers had known this struggle, and their grandfathers, and their great and great-great-grandfathers. This was life, and with resignation they accepted it. Yet within them surged constantly the craving to overpower these sinister forces. They tried to avoid them by trickery; they attempted to gain their favour through chants and offerings and rituals; and they sought to frustrate their wicked activities by appealing to a more powerful demon, called a wise-one, who was on a higher stratum of demon hierarchy and could induce submission and obedience from the lower-level demons.

Every Tadyawan tribesman, man or woman, coveted possession of a wise-one, but to only a few was the privilege granted, for demons appeared only to the tribesmen they chose. Bilbino's wife had merely attained to dealings with the lower-level demons; Bilbino went one step beyond, having his own wise-one, though impotent. Aplaki, however, was befriended by a very powerful wise-one, one that could foretell the weather or the evil intentions of men or demons. It forewarned of coming disaster and effectively avenged the wrongs inflicted by Aplaki's enemy tribesmen. It bestowed on Aplaki power to heal even the most serious illnesses. For his wise-one's helpful service Aplaki had only in return to obey all that the wise-one said. The arrangement was uncomplicated and beneficial, because Aplaki's fellow-tribesmen, then, appealed to him for mediation and healing, in return promising obedience to all that he said.

The more supernatural power he obtained from his wise-one the greater his following and the more powerful he became. While in some areas these power-invested men were terrifying political leaders, Aplaki proved the opposite. He was a good leader, satisfied with friendly agreements and never overdemanding. The Tadyawan tribesmen, and Bilbino especially, respected him for what he was and for what he had attained.

Bilbino's wife sought to resume their conversation that had silenced into long thoughtful meditation. "What else did Aplaki say?"

"About what?" asked Bilbino, his mind preoccupied.

"About our little daughter. Will he remove the thorns implanted in her leg by the demons? She has cried lots today from the pain."

"Oh, that! Yes, tomorrow. He said he'd perform the leaf ceremony too, to see if that would help."

"How early will you go?"

"As soon as the chickens come down from their roosts."

"I wonder if those foreign teachers will know how to heal sicknesses."

"He didn't say anything about that."

"When will they come?"

"When Aplaki is dead," answered Bilbino, and then he withdrew into serious thought again. How long *would* it be before they came?

Three years later he dared to hope it would be soon, for a Tadyawan friend arrived at his house and casually informed him of the latest mountain news.

4 Enmeshed

Bilbino's wife was just lifting the lid, bare-fingered, from
the black pot of steaming hot sweet potatoes when a
Tadyawan friend appeared in the doorway, blocking the
early morning light. He lurched his way through the
opening and sank into the big rattan swing strung up
beside where Bilbino was sitting on the floor, making
rattan snares. A dozen or more snares lay finished on the
floor beside him, the makings of many more at his feet.
Bilbino had been hungry for a good bird feast for a long
time and was now incited to action by the berries
beginning to appear on the trees.

Hardly in the swing, the new arrival removed the
woven purse-like pouch that dangled from around his
neck and lifted off its woven cover. From within he
reached for a bit of leaf and flattened it out on his bare
thigh. He dug into the pouch again for his small
container of lime and rubbed some on the leaf. Another
dig into the pouch and he produced a broken bit of betel
nut. This he folded in the limed leaf and then popped the
whole thing into his mouth. His chew safely lodged in his
cheek, he turned to Bilbino.

"You must have been cold last night," he joked.

Bilbino grinned, having caught the tone, and at the
same time brushed off some of the telltale ashes from his
legs and arms. The mountain air had been unusually cold
the night before and he had rolled into the fire-place as
far as he dared in order to supplement the little bit of
warmth his flour-sacking blanket offered him. The ashes
on his body spoke louder than any thermometer.

Bilbino's wife took some of the breakfast potatoes and placed them in a little woven basket and, with just a nod toward the friend, handed the basket to her skinny little son, whose eyes were so dark it was hard to tell where the pupil ended and the iris began. He was a chatterbox like his mother. Taking one look at the friend, he made a start for him. His older sister, another prankster, stretched her leg in front of him, feigning to trip him. He sidestepped her, giggling, and then darted toward the visitor, shoving the basket at him and unashamedly dashing back for his own share of the potatoes.

The visitor glanced at the food but never touched it, for he had no intention of wastefully spitting out his freshly-made chew of betel nut just to eat a few potatoes. Though he had hiked far, he wasn't hungry, and the betel taste in his mouth was satisfying; his salivary glands were responding nicely. Bending over and aiming dead-on, he spat the excess saliva through the slats of bamboo, the red mixture splattering on the ground below.

"Did you hear the dogs the other night?"

"Whose dogs?" inquired Bilbino, jerking his head but not his eyes in the direction of the friend in the swing.

"The Filipinos' from the town. A group of them arrived late in the evening, wanting to spend the night with us. They were hunting for wild pig and deer, but they didn't know their way around the forest and wanted one of us to guide them about. They ate at our place—made us kill two of our chickens so they'd have something to eat with the rice they had brought along."

"Did you kill the chickens?"

"Sure, we were afraid of their guns. They gave us a little coconut shell full of their cooked rice." And Bilbino and his friend laughed dryly at the unjust exchange.

"'Did anyone go with them?"

"Of course! Andoy. They had asked him directly, and he was afraid to say no." He paused and spat accurately again. "They said they'd pay him."

"And did they?"

"No, just some cigarettes. They were gone four days; passed through again last night."

The two men laughed again, attempting to disguise their anger and disgust. The laugh dislodged the betel nut, but the friend went right on talking unintelligibly, the words being blocked by the displaced quid and a tongue frantically trying to shove the chew back in the left cheek where it belonged. Bilbino asked for a repetition of what he had said.

"Lots of planes going over these days; folks in our community are worried. They think that the war our great-grandfathers predicted is near."

"Friend," Bilbino reassured, "you know the Tawbuid tribesmen deep in the interior of our mountains have offered us asylum when the war comes. Aplaki knows the way. He'll take us."

"But Aplaki is no more. He's rolled over."

"When?" Bilbino evidenced only a small measure of shock.

"A couple of days ago. I met one of his sons on the trail the other morning when I was out checking my pig traps for game, and he told me his dad had rolled over. They all left the house while his body was still warm."

"Were they afraid?"

"Not very much, for Aplaki was a good man, and his wise-one had promised to take him to a good place when he died. His family is sure that his soul was taken up to the stars. He was too good to turn into an evil spirit."

Bilbino's wife in selfishly mournful tones interrupted, "Who will be our leader now?"

"I don't know," both men simultaneously answered, and they were honest. Who in these mountains nearby had as much power as Aplaki had had? Who knew how to release an imprisoned soul from the baskets of the demons? Who would warn them when their enemies cursed them? Who would chant for fertility for the women whom the demons had doomed to sterility? Who would drive away the demons that made their children hot-tempered? When their fields were overrun by hungry rats and wild pigs, who would entreat for them to be run off into another area? Who would break the demons' jinx on their traps? Who would lift the curse when a man violated one of the multitudinous taboos? Yes, who? Where would they find another leader like Aplaki?

Bilbino's mind pondered the problem later that day as he walked from tree to tree tying his snares on the branches right in front of a tempting cluster of berries. Only one little solace stabbed the worry: Now that Aplaki was dead, maybe those strangers would soon be coming.

How soon? He could only hope very soon, for if life had been difficult before, it would be even more so now until they found a replacement for Aplaki. It had to be someone who could deal with the demons and spirits, someone with an informative and helpful wise-one, and someone to pacify those ugly-tempered tribesmen whose only language for gaining their own ends was brutality. "Maybe the coming strangers would be able to handle those brazen ones," Bilbino encouraged himself.

That little hope would spare them complete despair through the next years as Bilbino and his friends plodded on under the heat of terror and toil, tempered only with short snatches of happiness in a good crop, game in the trap, a catch of fish.

But soon after Aplaki's death Bilbino and his wife

shared a secret which they jealously guarded. As they dared not let the demons overhear a conversation about the arrival of another child, they never mentioned it—not even to the members of their own household. But Bilbino's relatives were sharp and quick and before long noticed Bilbino's wife observing some of the taboos incumbent on all expectant mothers. They respected her right to secrecy, however, and never discussed their suspicions among themselves lest demon ears profit from the information and harm either her or the baby. Only as the time drew near did they allow themselves a few short and hurried whispers.

When the day for delivery had obviously come, Bilbino and his wife, her face showing signs of its imminence, left the large household and went to one of the abandoned field huts. Bilbino banged the dust and dirt through the flooring of the tiny shelter and hastily whittled a piece of rattan into a very sharp edge. That job done, the delivery room and Dr. Bilbino were all set for the arrival of his child. Having had the experience twice already, he wasn't fearful or clumsy as at first. Confident, he successfully delivered a little girl. But there was another—a son! Twins! Both he and his wife grew fearful. This was a serious omen indeed, meaning death for his wife, or for the twins, or for all three.

Bilbino knew what he must do, and he wasted no time in doing it. A thin vine made into a noose, a pathetic whimper, and the little warm corpse of his newborn son lay across his knees. The demons were satisfied; Bilbino, relieved.

After discarding the baby boy's body among the roots of some trees, he attended to his duties for his new daughter. Taking her umbilical cord, he wrapped it in a leaf and tied it high in a tree bordering on one of their fields, knowing that this would insure her being an industrious worker when she grew up and thus desired for a wife, freeing him from having to support her.

In the following years other children were born into their family. Some died because of sickness; others lived in spite of it. In the outside world, war was going on and the Japanese invaded their island. Yet they stayed secure in their mountains, with only their own local problems enmeshing them. Bilbino's problems grew with his family, for the larger the family, the more time he was forced to spend dealing with the demons and the ancestors' spirits, as somebody was always sick, be it a son or daughter, a son-in-law, or a grandchild. The demons of that area were legion. Bilbino couldn't cope. Though he tried all the methods, he could gain no access to a wise-one stronger than the limited one who visited him. Was there another area, he wondered, where the demons were fewer and where the neighbours would be kinder than their present ones? He knew they could not stay there much longer. They would have to run away.

5 An Attempt to Escape

"How was it?" his wife asked after Bilbino and one of his sons-in-law had settled their chilled bodies down beside the fireplace.

Bilbino, slowly massaging his aching body, studied his feet and replied evasively, "There was lots of rain."

She was secretly pleased. The absence of a negative

answer encouraged her to believe that they had found some land they could all move to. But she wisely prodded no further, just as anxious as her husband that the demons know nothing of their contemplated move. Instead she felt in the palm-leaf wall for the blackened salmon tin and filled it with water from the bamboo tube, then into the can she dropped the little shrimp that the men had hand-caught on their way home up the stream. She placed the can securely in the fire and grabbed her unfinished wicker basket, light-heartedly weaving and chattering away the news of the past few days: her knife blade had flown off its handle and over her head the other day when she was chopping wood; Dolilaw had fallen at the stream and cut her hand on the water gourd that she was carrying; and their eldest son had chopped down his first tree under the supervisory shouts and encouragements of the rest of the family.

"If somebody hadn't helped him, you wouldn't see us today, for he would have felled it right on to the house," she added teasingly, squinting at her young son. Everybody in the house laughed again at the recollection of it, while the boy sat studying the fire, pretending to be deaf to the whole conversation.

"He'll soon learn," Bilbino comforted, chortling at the thought of his short and skinny son already aspiring to manhood.

There was a lull. His wife changed the subject.

"Those brazen ones are at it again."

"Oh, whom did they beat this time?" Fear rose deep within Bilbino.

"Santoy," his wife said, "or Santoy's brother. I'm not sure; neither was the one who told me the news."

"Why did they beat him?"

She scratched her head, then gave it a thud with her

palm to make the lice stop annoying her and, laughing, she replied, "He killed one of their men."

"That's a lie! How did he kill him?"

"He was talking to the man just a day or two before the man died. They claimed it was all that talking that made him so sick that he died.

"They demanded a pig—but he didn't want to give them the only pig the family had, so he refused. They beat him right there in his own home. His shoulders are so bruised that he can't work in the fields yet."

The conversation accelerated Bilbino's thinking. Now that they had found some land, they must move as soon as possible. It didn't matter if the first year or so would be difficult until the land produced; they just had to get away from those wicked men and from the demons and spirits.

He moved over closer to his wife and whispered in her ear what he hadn't wanted to mention earlier for fear they had been followed home by demons undetected. He hadn't really seen any coming along the path behind them, nor in the grass, but then he nor anyone was ever perfectly sure. "The Pola River area is a good place," he confided. "The land looks good for crops; the people are friendly and welcome us; the demons are at a minimum, they say; and the Tawbuid tribesmen are very close by in case we ever need them for their powerful medicine against the demons. The people say the Tawbuid are happy to perform the ceremonies just as long as they are paid well."

"How soon can we go?" she asked hopefully, eager to get away from trouble.

"I don't know," drawled Bilbino, calculating at the same time just how soon someone could go over and build a new house and get some of the land cleared for next year's crops. At the same time, all the work would have to be carried on there at home so they wouldn't go hungry. He wagered a guess, however: "Maybe the next rainy season."

At the end of the summer when the bright, exhilarating days of warmth and sunshine succumbed to greyness, wetness and mould, they were ready to go. Land in the Pola area, broken by Bilbino's vanguard, already held in its good soil the beginnings of a sweet potato crop; and a small house, easily added to later, beckoned their occupation. Only one thing detained them, the moon. To move at the time of the new moon, when the uninterrupted darkness would offer them a continual screen as they escaped from their demon enemies, was the safest plan.

Bilbino studied carefully the positions of the moon, and then one morning informed the family in cautiously subdued tones, "We'll be moving in about four nights, I think. Everybody must be ready to go in the middle of the night. Don't save your packing-up till then, but get it all done beforehand during the day. We can't afford to disturb the demons from their sleep, for they'll know immediately what we're up to, and they'll make plans to follow us. If they follow us, you know the Pola Tadyawan will not allow us into their area. We've all got to be careful. We'll travel in small groups and meet at the head of the stream on the next mountain and then proceed together from there."

With little comment the household suppressed the news and didn't discuss it again, except when necessary, and then made only vague allusions to it. On the scheduled night they carried on with supper as usual, hiding their anxiety by forced nonchalant chatter. All around them, though, the house was stripped and already looked unlived-in. No leftover bits of frog or monkey meat hung on poles over the fireplace; all tuck-away places in the walls and roof were destitute of fishing goggles, slingshots, odd bits of rags, old tin cans salvaged from civilization's scrap heap, and other odd treasures. Earlier that day all those things had been carefully stuffed into the wicker baskets that were now propped against poles of the house or the walls. The rattan swing, bent in half and tied securely, lay on the floor, its leaf lining concealing its contents of potatoes and cassava, ready to be carried south for the first few meals. No chickens or roosters were tethered to poles in the corners of the house, for they had been enclosed, but not without their objecting squawks, in wicker baskets to be toted by the younger children. Everything looked ready.

They all settled down early that night, one by one stretching out on the floor, pretending to anticipate a good night's sleep. The children and teenagers slept soundly, but the older ones were restless, waiting for Bilbino's signal to get on the move.

In the middle of the quiet forest night Bilbino silently sat up, his wife just as silently following; then one or two more; then more until the whole house was engaged in stealthy activity, folding their blankets and soundlessly jamming them into the sides of the packed baskets. Mothers scooped up their babies, blankets and all, and set them in big wicker baskets, leaving the babies' heads to totter until they found the ridge of the basket and, supported by it, went off to sleep again. When some of the women got a bit excited and let out a few words to their husbands, the husbands gave them no encouragement—this was the serious moment.

Without any light, small groups of two or three slipped out of the house into the dead silence of the moonless night. They were familiar with the trails near home and had no fear of straying in the darkness. It was better not to light a torch lest it alert the demons. They travelled up the small streams that flowed down over mountain rock, for demons couldn't climb waterfalls and, if, perchance, any were accidentally around and started to follow, they would soon lose them.

Their getaway was done to perfection, for though they were many in number, the human ear could not detect the tread of their bare feet. Only occasionally they were made conscious of each other by the snap of a twig as they headed in the direction of their rendezvous. Arriving, many of them sighed with quiet relief at having gone that far without any sign of demon knowledge. Some of the more daring even muffled a "three cheers" with triumphant eyes set in poker faces.

As it was safe now to have a light, Bilbino lit some resin which had been bound tightly in long, slender leaves. Once the torch was burning freely, he held it high and took a silent census of the group.

"Where's my little Dolilaw?" he asked, restraining anxiety.

Nobody knew.

"She must have taken the wrong path on the trail. Who was walking behind her?"

Nobody knew.

Bilbino's mind travelled quickly. "Who was the one who woke her up back at the house?"

Nobody knew. Could it be? Yes, they unanimously concluded, Dolilaw must still be back at the house. What a waste of a perfect escape! They knew that by that time she had probably awakened and, terrified at being all alone, was screaming her head off, unconsciously announcing to the demons that they had gone. If anyone went back to rescue her, the demons would assuredly follow them. There was no other recourse; they would all have to go back and wait for another time to make the move.

Back the party went, tittering away their keen disappointment. They couldn't afford to be angry; the demons would know and then punish Dolilaw with sickness. No, this was fate; they'd have to try again at a later moon. Carefully retracing their steps, they arrived back at the house to find Dolilaw still curled up under her blanket sound asleep over by the wall.

The next time they scheduled their move to the Pola River area they made sure all the children were up and moving before the last adult left the house. Success marked this venture, and they arrived safely in the darkness of the early morning, weary yet exultant in their achievement. Bilbino lit a new torch, held it high in his hand and circled the house with it while he chanted to the unknown good spirit, invoking blessing for a safe and happy existence in this their new home. Life was beginning again!

6 The Strangers

Bilbino and clan stayed in the Pola River area for many years. The demons and spirits, if they were indeed fewer, continued to be a menace and to batter down their zest for life. But in spite of it the family liked it there, for the neighbours were both good and helpful.

Grandchildren now played in the clearing, alternately amusing and worrying the ageing Bilbino. With all the passing years, however, Bilbino had not forgotten the prediction of Aplaki's vision that good people would come with good teaching. But would they really come, he puzzled, or was the whole thing a trick of the demons?

Bilbino mentioned it to one of his Pola neighbours one day. "Oh, but they're here!" the neighbour replied. "They've been here for a long time. They wear white robes, and everybody calls them Father. We see them when we go into town. They're kind to us and give us rations of clothing and rice and sardines if we go into town on the appointed day. You come to town with us, and you'll get some too. They invited us to their big house to pray."

Bilbino and his son-in-law, Pedro, weren't at all convinced. The spirit-being had said the strangers would come into the mountains.

"You go and see them; surely they are the ones you mean," urged the friend.

"No," contradicted Bilbino; "it couldn't be; we'll wait for the other strangers."

And they waited—for a long time yet. And while they waited, civilization was getting closer and closer, all kinds of civilization, the kind and the unkind, the swindlers and the honest. Filipinos from overcrowded islands were beginning to come to Mindoro in quest of land, any land, even land in the mountains. Gradually they were settling in, here one, there one; and gradually, too, tribespeople with an insatiable thirst for learning conquered fears of taboos and ventured out to the outside world to view its progress and to see what profit was there for themselves.

Bilbino's wife was sitting outside her house one day pounding with the blunt edge of her knife on a piece of bark that she had peeled from a tree earlier that day. She was making a new loincloth, dampening the bark with water, then pounding, then repeating the process until she was satisfied that it was soft and pliable like a piece of loosely woven material. Above the *thunk, thunk* of her pounding she heard the roar of a motor, close.

"There they are," she called to the others in the house. "There are those Filipinos again at their sawmill. They'll soon be chopping down all the big trees around here. I hope they don't come in this far. I don't want them in here. Somebody told me they have a lot of trucks."

"They say," Pedro's wife added, "that they've got somebody there who gives medicine—through a big long needle which they stick into people. Not me, ever!"

"We women had better stay away from there anyway. Remember what's-his-name's wife said that those men have evil thoughts toward tribal women. They are stronger than we are."

"Yes, let's let the men go there to visit, not us," agreed Pedro's wife.

Though many of them were fearful at first, the men did go out increasingly often. The Filipinos who were opening up land wanted cheap help. And eager to earn a little cash, tribesmen overcame their natural timidity and lent themselves out as labourers. They didn't know the value of the cash they earned, they just knew that with it they could purchase things at the canteen on the sawmill grounds like the Filipinos did.

It was hard-earned cash, though, chopping down trees a whole day and then collecting twenty-five *centavos*, if they were lucky. For often their would-be employer wouldn't pay them at all, pretending he had inadvertently left his money at his other house in town. Always at the mercy of demons or men, life for them was cruel. But the Lord delights in mercy to the oppressed. He had not forgotten them!

"I've seen something very strange today," informed one of the men who had just returned from the sawmill. With that announcement he had everyone's attention.

"They said they were women," he continued, "and they looked like women; but I'm not so sure they were. They had light hair and light eyes, and their skin was pale. When they talked to each other, it was just like birds twittering."

Bilbino was deeply interested.

The man went on: "They were teaching from some papers, lots of them all sewn together. They said they got their teachings from those papers, and those papers were from 'Our Father' up there in heaven."

"Was it good teaching?" Bilbino interrupted.

"Yes, it was good, like the great-grandfathers taught us. But I didn't stay around long. They were frightening to see."

"Surely," concluded Bilbino, "these are the strange people we've been looking for. They have come to our mountains. This is what Aplaki's spirit-being was talking about." And he was as excited as a Tadyawan tribesman ever gets.

"No, I don't think so," the man contradicted, quelling Bilbino's excitement a bit. "I think they're demons out of the ground, because their stench is strong, just like the demons. They couldn't really be people."

Though the others in the large family were very much frightened over this news, Bilbino and his son-in-law Pedro wanted to see the women for themselves. They had been waiting too long a time to dismiss the matter now with a word from someone else.

Sometime later another man came home saying that he had seen the women in his travels in the mountains and that they were carrying a little wooden box with shiny

black things—round, thin, and flat—that talked when the
women turned a handle. "The words were good words,"
the messenger exclaimed.

"Where do they live?" asked Bilbino hopefully.

"I don't know—far away north, I think," conjectured
the man.

Bilbino said no more, but inwardly hoped his chance
to see the women would be soon.

And it was.

7 Bilbino Sees for Himself

Bilbino looked at his young grandson lying on the floor
atop a piece of ragged burlap and at the same time threw
on to the fire the smouldering stick of wood which he had
just finished waving over his grandson's body.

"Feel better?" he inquired of the lad, who was about
ten dry seasons old.

Young Mabilis kept his eyes closed and only slightly
shifted his thin body, limp with fever. Moving pained his
ulcerated leg, and he winced but uttered no cry of pain.

"No." It was all he could manage to say.

Bilbino frowned in despair. Why shouldn't the demons
respond to his chantings? Just which demon had bitten
Mabilis and caused this huge ulcer, raging red and
sickeningly infected? His little body was getting thinner
and thinner. Though Bilbino had placated every demon
he knew, calling them by name, they had ignored his
pleas. He had tried the spirits of the ancestors. What
next? Wasn't Mabilis going to get well again? Maybe he

should try a method of medicine he had learned from the Tawbuid tribesmen, the chant to the anonymous demon. He felt sure he remembered the magical words and the chant. He determined to try it.

"Get me a *mimali* branch," he snapped at his youngest son Bisi, his sharp eyes demanding immediate response. Bisi obeyed, and the branch was lying at Bilbino's feet in just a few lightnings of the fireflies.

Bilbino took the branch and held it over the fire. Being still green, it didn't burn, but became steadily hotter. Bilbino kept his eye on it; and when he felt it had reached the appropriate temperature, he removed it from the fire and broke the stem. It steamed. Good! It was what he had hoped for. He held the steaming branch over Mabilis's body while he muttered the magical words and then chanted to the unknown demon:

> "Go back to whoever owns you.
> Do not bite Mabilis any more.
> Go, bite somebody else."

Chant finished, he tossed the branch aside and looked for improvement in Mabilis. But Mabilis felt the same. He was completely spent from the fever and the throbbing in his leg. Bilbino was frustrated. "Maybe the demons have imprisoned his soul," he sighed uneasily.

"Yes, maybe; or eaten it," added one of the household matter-of-factly.

But to the serious little lad on the floor there was nothing matter-of-fact about it. He was worried; he knew what it meant to have one's soul eaten. Would he see tomorrow? he wondered. Or would he be—where would he be?

But Mabilis did see tomorrow, in fact, a good many tomorrows. His ulcer, however, was no better, his fever

no lower, and his fears no less. Bilbino would make one
final attempt to gain his healing. As leader now of his
family group, he *had* to, or lose their respect and with it
his prestige.

"Let's take Mabilis down to that sawmill for one of
those needles," was his suggestion.

"Not me!" chorused most of the household. "I don't
want to go there. I'm afraid of those Filipinos."

"Maybe they'll inject something into him that will kill
him right there at the sawmill," someone wailed. "Oh,
don't take him there!"

"Yes, we should try," insisted Bilbino. "My older
brother heard about a Filipino lady who got needles for
her ulcer, and it healed completely. She is still alive and
sells eggplant at the sawmill. I think we should take
Mabilis down and see."

"I'll go with you," volunteered Mabilis's stepfather.

"Me too," added Pedro eagerly. "I'd like to see how
they do it."

Bilbino was hoping Pedro would go, as the progressive
young man had been learning a lot of the Filipino
language and could explain what they wanted.

"What about payment?" Bilbino asked. "Who's got
some of those *cinkos*?"

There was a scuffling as the men felt around in their
rattan pouches for the five-*centavo* pieces and the women
took off their necklaces to search. The pouches yielded a
few coins, and the women found a few others among the
animal teeth, bells, and fetishes wrapped in pieces of
dark, dirty cloth that hung around their necks. From the
grubby string they slid off all the paraphernalia until they
reached the pierced *cinkos* and then slipped these treasures
off too, cheerfully surrendering them for the cause.

Bilbino looked at the small collection of coins. He

hadn't any real idea of their composite value but estimated that they were too few.

"That's not enough," he said. "We'd better hunt for an orchid and take that along too. My older brother tells me that the Filipinos like orchids and will pay money for them. We could sell one and use the money for the injection."

Pedro stretched for his jungle knife that was lying in its sheath on top of a pile of newly split firewood someone had carried into the house. He straightened his back, expanding his chest while he tied the vine cord of the sheath around his waist. After sucking some food from between his rotting teeth, he edged over to the doorway. "I won't be long," he said.

Out in the forest, walking along partly overgrown foot trails, his eyes searched the trees. Looking for a parasitic green plant against a whole background of green was only for the trained. But he was trained. He found one without flowers, hearty and lush, growing high up in one of the trees, quite well off the path. He seized his knife and hacked his way through the brush to the tree, climbed it, and cut away the plant, taking care not to lop off any of its precious long branches, each resembling a cat's tail, thick with soft green needles. "This should sell for some *cinkos,*" he gloated, pleased with his find.

Early the next morning, with the five-*centavo* pieces tied tightly in a rag and the orchid tied to a pole for over-the-shoulder carrying, they were ready to go, a party of five: Bilbino, Pedro, young Bisi, the patient Mabilis, and Mabilis's stepfather.

"We'll go now," they announced to the others after they had leaf-wrapped some cold leftover rice for lunch along the way.

"All right," was the reply. "Go carefully."

Their excited chatter echoed back as they disappeared down the trail, Mabilis hobbling along behind them, relying heavily on his walking stick.

Suddenly the stepfather tripped on a root sticking out of the ground, a root which he hadn't seen, so busy was he talking. "That's it," he said and immediately turned around and headed for the house again. No one questioned him. They all knew that the spirits were trying to stop him from going. He had to comply or cope with their retaliation. He chose to comply.

"Be careful going back," they said as they continued on down the mountain.

Having carried Mabilis over the roughest spots, the group stepped out of the thick forest about an hour later into the bright sunshine of the Pola River valley. The Pola was nearly always a mad river in spate, but this time of year it was beautifully clear, lazily flowing over the stones.

Though the Tadyawan were excited over this their first real business adventure with the outside world, the nearer they got to the sawmill, the more fearful they became. Thoughts clamoured within them: Would the people listen to them? Would they understand Pedro's attempts to speak in the Filipino language? Would the lowlanders make fun of them in their loincloths? Maybe they would just take their money and not give Mabilis the needle. Their mounting fears were real, and enough to make them want to go back home again; but Bilbino's fear of losing his grandson and his power as a leader was even greater. So on they went, hoping that somehow they would win the day.

But it never entered Bilbino's mind at that moment that his hopes of a lifetime were about to be realized— that his own eyes would finally see the strangers that

Aplaki's spirit-visitor had foretold would come; he would meet them at the sawmill.

Having no idea that *we* were the long-looked-for strangers, Hazel Page and I sat wearily at the sawmill battling with our emotions. We were tired and hot; we needed a bath, and we longed for a good night's sleep between clean, cool sheets. During the past three days we had been trekking in the mountains and on the plains, living out of our army packs and sleeping on hard, wooden floors, all the time hoping to find tribespeople. But the tribespeople had an uncanny way of remaining elusive. We had seen very few on that trip, and then for only scattered minutes. They were too frightened of us bleached-looking creatures to want to stay around us for very long.

It was then 1955, and the Overseas Missionary Fellowship was still new in the Philippines. Though we felt responsible under God to evangelize the tribespeople who inhabited the uplands of Mindoro Island, we knew little about them. History books did mention them, but exactly how many tribes were secluded in the mountain forests or where their boundaries were, nobody seemed to know. According to the books, these primitive peoples migrated to the islands centuries ago, filing down the Malayan Peninsula from the eastern part of the Asian continent and using the islands of what is now Indonesia as stepping stones to the Philippines. Later, more advanced, more aggressive Malays arrived, pushing the early settlers off the plains and into the mountains. By the time we arrived on the scene, the mountain dwellers made contact with the outside world only when they themselves got courage to venture out to civilization; civilization seldom found them, for they kept their trails undefined and purposely obscured to keep outsiders out. So to find them, we had to hunt for them. Hazel and I made up one of several survey teams that went on these manhunts, following up any information we got concerning the whereabouts of these timid people.

On the porch of an unpainted, tumbledown building, on a wooden bench beside a door with "Office" chalked on it, we sat that day wondering about our technique. We seemed to be doing a lot of hunting and not much finding. Discouraged and quiet with fatigue, we were waiting in hopes of hitching a ride on a logging truck going out to the main road nine miles away. While offering nothing in comfort, a ride on one of those relics of World War II was preferable to hiking on the airless, open road. As we waited, tough lumbermen strode in and out of the office door, our presence drawing their stares and provoking undertoned conversations.

We looked at our watches. It was getting late, and there was no sign of any truck going out of camp. If we were going to have to walk the nine miles, we knew we would have to leave soon or we would never make it out to the main road in time to catch the last bus home. But the prospect of that long walk in the still heat of the late afternoon made us linger at the sawmill just a bit longer. Quietly and aimlessly we sat watching the rusty crane lifting logs off trucks and swinging them over to the large mound of logs awaiting sawing. And then suddenly into our sawmill landscape stepped four tribesmen in loincloths. They appeared on the crest of a high mound of hot sawdust, paused, then made their way around the shell of a building that housed a screeching saw, and stepped on to the path that led to the building marked "Office".

Coming toward the building, they suddenly saw us and

stopped dead. We held our breath, wondering if they would turn around and run away. Our army packs lay at our feet, right in our path of advance. We managed, however, carefully to kick them out of the way, at the same time reaching for the phonograph and records we had brought with us. Then with forced composure so as not to frighten the four, we descended the rickety steps and approached them smiling. Handsome Bilbino shied away, taking shelter behind Pedro, who bore the orchid over his shoulder. Pedro boasted no natural beauty. His teeth were irregular and rotted, his eyes were crossed, and his head bore a thick crop of uncontrolled hair. Obviously on guard, yet inquisitive, Pedro listened to what we were struggling to say in Tagálog. We knew nothing of their Tadyawan language and were only beginners in the Filipino language.

Had they ever heard of "Our Father" up there in heaven? No answer. Our Father is the One who made everything, including them. Still no comment. The tribesmen just stared, their eyes glued on our persons, but never lifting to meet our eyes. "These papers have Our Father's words on them," we went on. "He wants everybody to hear them because He tells in them how people can get to His good house when they die. Would you like to hear some of His words?"

"How much did your shoes cost?" asked Pedro.

Oh, groan! "Four *pesos*," we hastily answered, and with the same breath quickly added, "Would you like to hear some of Our Father's words from this phonograph?"

They looked at the box suspiciously. Not waiting for a "no" or a "yes", we opened the phonograph, wound it quickly, and slipped a record on the spindle, talking during the whole process lest we lose our audience. The inside of the phonograph fascinated them. We played a record in the Filipino language, and they seemed to like it. Then we casually got out a record that had been made some years previously by Gospel Recordings missionaries who had come to Mindoro to record the tribal languages through interpreters. This record was marked "Tribes of Pola"; so we played it, not having any idea what the record said or if it was said in the language of the people standing around us. As the jerky sentences spilled out, Pedro dug his tongue into his hollow teeth, shooting a grimace at Bilbino. Bilbino covered a big grin with his hand, his eyes sparkling over the top. We knew we were on familiar ground.

"Did you understand that?" we asked, already positive that the record was in their language.

"No," they lied. "We're going now." And as abruptly as they had come into our lives, they left to tend to their own affairs, leaving us deflated and wondering if we would ever see them again. We had had so many contacts like this one—short and interesting, yet never producing anything—that again we wondered if there weren't some other way to launch the church-planting work we had come to do. But we couldn't find another way. We knew we would have to go on trekking, making brief contacts, praying and waiting for the Lord's fullness of time for a welcome among the tribes. We did not then know that His time for Bilbino's clan was still five years away and that in the interim we would have that heart-breaking experience at Katubo's.

8 Another Move—and Ben

Pedro and Bilbino returned to their mountain home with the younger boys, reasonably proud of their accomplishments at the sawmill. The rest of the family shot questions at them rapid-fire: Did Mabilis get the injection? Did it hurt? Where did they stick the needle in? Were the Filipinos kind?

Their animated conversation, interspersed with shouts of laughter, continued until Bilbino, still talking, reached into his dirty brown cloth sack and extracted from it a small white paper bag—at least, it had been white earlier. Conversation stopped short. All eyes were on the bag; the children huddled around. Bilbino laid the bag on the floor and then tore it open, exposing to all the crumbled remains of some crackers he had bought at the sawmill canteen. He handed bits of the crackers to the children, who flew in all directions distributing them until everybody in the house had a piece. Some smelled it; some licked it; some ran the crumb along their arms. The children held theirs, with eyes on their parents. Was it to eat? Most of them waited for the nibbles of the venturesome few and dared to taste only after the nibblers grimaced acceptance, but all agreed that crackers were not to be compared with the familiar sweet potatoes and rice.

When the cracker bits were all out of sight, Bilbino threw the torn paper bag to the children, who played with it and then fought over the crumpled treasure.

Bilbino addressed the adults: "We've seen those women whom what's-his-name saw a couple of months ago."

"What women? You mean the demons who look like white women?"

"No, they aren't demons; they are real people, just like us. We were talking to them. Their teaching is good."

"You'd better be careful," warned Bilbino's wife, whose pretty face was adding wrinkles speedily and whose laughter was becoming a lusty cackle. "Remember what your cousin said about some white women many years ago who came here to teach, and then when that war broke out and the Japanese came, they went back to their country and brought over some of their men, who captured lots of tribesmen and carried them off to war."

It was a nagging thought. They had heard the tale before. The men smiled weakly. Pedro's wife shot fearful eyes at him and said, "The Tadyawan east of here said those women would build a big stone house and lock all our children in it and make them study. We don't want our children taken away from us." Her tone was threatening. She clutched the vine attached to the hammock and gave a little tug to set the hammock swaying, reassuring her only child, a baby boy, that she was still near.

So during the following weeks, the joy of watching Mabilis recuperate and begin to enter enthusiastically into boyish pranks again was dulled by a new worry, the worry expressed by Pedro's wife.

It would be an awful thing to have their children taken away from them. But would *those* women do it? They had been kind that day. Pedro and Bilbino had felt sure they were the long-awaited strangers, the ones that the spirit had said would come. They hoped to see them again sometime and listen to more of that teaching.

A few more years went by, adding more wrinkles to the

elderly, more brawn to the young men, and more work for the growing family ever over-shadowed with the increasing fears of demons and men and sickness and death. They had so much sickness in this place that again Bilbino was faced with a decision: it was time for another move.

"Find a place where there aren't any demons," he demanded of Pedro and another of his sons-in-law, whom he had deployed as a search party.

Where on that whole island could such a place be found? They searched often and for long periods of time until one day, when they were far south on the Banos River, they stumbled on to some Tawbuid tribesmen fishing in a stream. They stood and watched for many minutes before they dared to approach these unfriendly, tall fellows intent on their fishing.

"Friends, do you live here?" asked Pedro, who had learned a good bit of the Tawbuid language.

"No," a Tawbuid replied abruptly, continuing to search the stream for fish, lifting a rock here, now there, hands poised ready to pounce down on anything that might be hidden behind the rock.

"Who owns all this land then?" asked Pedro sucking air through his front teeth.

"We do," said the Tawbuid spokesman, straightening his back and poking around in his clogged-up pipe.

"I guess there are lots of demons and spirits here," ventured Pedro's companion.

"No, not now," assured the Tawbuid man. "We used to live here, and we cursed this land so that the demons wouldn't come up out of the ground any more."

Now *there* was news! Pedro and his brother-in-law were highly interested. "Well, who lives here now then?"

"Nobody."

"We'll buy this land from you," Pedro proposed.

"What'll you give us?"

"What do you want?"

"One pig, one axe, and some knives," the Tawbuid replied, hitting his pipe against his palm and then poking in it some more.

"All right. We'll tell our leader. He'll meet you here the next full moon, and you can talk it over and make an agreement."

An agreement was accomplished, and another secret move was made—this time south to the Banos.

Here the large family of children and grandchildren started all over again, once more indulging in a hope that life would be more tolerable, free from the taunts of the demons and spirits at least, if not from men. To the west of them lived the aloof and fearsome Tawbuid, notorious for their powers to curse people. To the east lay the hilly slopes already occupied by the advancing Filipinos, who were forced to brave the rigours of mountain life because no land in the plains was left for claiming.

A Filipino neighbour of theirs, and an amicable one, was Ben. His black curly hair topped a round, pleasant face that broke into a smile easily. The Tadyawan liked Ben, his friendly manner and his easy-going style. He had a home in Pinamalayan, one of the big towns on the plain, but had come into the mountains to find himself some land to raise a rice crop to supplement his income. He needed the tribesmen's help in clearing the land and in caring for the growing crop when he was down in the town. Asking Pedro if he would be responsible for his fields, he promised him part of the crop for his own. It was a satisfactory arrangement for both.

"I've just seen Ben again," Pedro informed Bilbino at the start of another dry season. "He wants us to work his field this year like we did last year, and he'll give us some of the rice again."

"He's a kind one, that one," remarked Bilbino happily. "He always pays us what he says he'll pay. What did you say the name of the town is where he lives?"

"Pinamalayan. That's right beside the sea." Pedro had been there a number of times. "Ben's house is a big one with lots of partitions. But the floors are not bamboo like ours, they're solid wood, hard to sleep on, and you can't spit anything through them. But it's good that Ben lets us sleep there in spite of the plank floor and the mosquitoes; it's better than sleeping on the sand beside the sea. You should go to town with us sometime."

"Not me," asserted Bilbino, whose inquisitiveness had never been intense enough to conquer his cowardice. He preferred the security of the mountains. The charms of the outside world never outweighed the terrors that it held for him. "Does Ben own all that land across the river?"

"No, not yet, but he hopes to some day," replied Pedro.

"There are many Filipinos coming in now, and they are all hunting for land. My older brother tells me that some of them have actually chased some of the tribesmen off their own land so that they could have it for themselves. Soon all the land will be taken by the Filipinos; then what about us? Did you hear what the big, fat Filipino said the other day when we passed the new house that he's put up, along the river? He said that he owns all this land on our side, including right where we are living, the land we paid the Tawbuid for. He says, though, that we can go on living on it for a while. Did you hear him holler at our cousin when he didn't get the firewood right away for him? He isn't kind like Ben. He told me that some of his friends were also coming in here for land. I guess that's why we see so many of them travelling along the river. I asked him to pity us, but he only laughed and said we could go further into the mountains and find land there. But the soil there is rocky and dry. We'll die of starvation," concluded Bilbino, distressed.

What an existence! If not demons, then men, and loss of their land, their one means of livelihood. What would be left? It was a hopeless picture except for one thing. "I asked Ben if he knew anything about those women," Pedro said.

"What did he say?" and tones got brighter again, particularly Bilbino's, who wanted to hear more of that teaching.

"He said, 'You mean those Americans?' And I said, 'We don't know who they are, but they have big noses, and they are white. They teach good things.'"

"He knew them, then?"

"He said he saw them once riding through Pinamalayan on a bus; so I asked him to bring them in here sometime. He said he would if ever he saw them again."

Ben didn't know when he made that promise to Pedro just how he'd fulfil it, but the "fullness of time" was fast approaching now, and Our Father knew how He would bring about the contact.

9 Escorted into the Mountains

Pinamalayan, Ben's town, had a mixed population. Scattered about the small nipa huts or the grand old Spanish frame homes of the Filipinos lived the rich

Chinese merchants. One of OMF's Chinese-speaking missionaries, Russell Glazier, was deeply concerned for these Chinese. And one day he and some of the Chinese young people from the city of Manila visited Pinamalayan.

They spoke of Christ to many that day—Chinese, and Filipinos too. In God's plan Mr. Glazier's path crossed Ben's. He gave Ben a tract and explained the gospel to him. Ben was open and friendly, but he felt he couldn't respond. "I am like the man you gave as an illustration," he said. "I'm in the boat wanting to launch out and believe, but I can't cut the rope that keeps me anchored to the dock. There are so many things I want in life. To believe would cost me too much."

"I'd like to pray for you," said Mr. Glazier.

"All right," came Ben's cheerful answer. "And say, by the way," he added, "do you by any chance have women in your mission who could teach tribespeople? There are some who live in the mountains near my farm, and they have asked me to accompany women teachers into their mountains to teach them."

"We do have some women teachers. I'll mention it to them when I go up north to Calapan," he assured Ben.

"They'll never be able to find the place in the mountains by themselves; so I'll take them in," offered Ben. "Just tell them to come down here to Pinamalayan, and we'll make arrangements for the trip." With a handshake and smiles they parted.

Arriving in Calapan, Mr. Glazier didn't forget his promise to Ben. Doris Pack and I were among those sitting at the dinner table in the mission home that night when he relayed Ben's message about the tribespeople near his farm. Both of us had been assigned by this time specifically to the Tadyawan tribe, and the area Mr.

Glazier described sounded like Tadyawan country. Conversation immediately picked up. *Tribespeople actually asking for someone to come in to teach them?* You could hardly blame Doris (whom I always called by her nickname, Dode) and me for getting excited. If these people were Tadyawan, maybe this was the wedge we had been persistently praying for! Maybe these were the people I had asked the Lord to prepare!

Itching to know the answers to the questions buzzing around in our heads, we lost no time in making an attempt to find out. The very next morning we hopped on to a red wooden bus bound for Pinamalayan, met Ben and his wife, and made arrangements for him to guide us into the mountains to meet his tribal friends.

The trip was one long walk, longer than we had counted on. At the outset, while we were still following the river on the wide plains, we enjoyed the view immensely. Fields of uncut rice bent over in heaviness under a gorgeous expanse of blue sky and against the background of the silent blue-green mountains that were our destination. But delays frustrated our eagerness to reach tribal territory. Ben was a surveyor by profession and had many friends all along the way on the plains. With him he carried a bottle—his method, he explained, for public relations. Maybe some day they would ask him to survey their land.

It being harvest time, all his friends whom we stopped by to see were extra busy. But if harvest made them extra busy, it also made them extra cheerful. Ben's bottle added greatly to their gaiety. They stopped whatever they were doing, whether threshing with their bare feet or winnowing with their flat woven trays or pounding in their homemade mortars. They all took time to be friendly. Each visit meant introductions, an explanation of who we were and what we were hoping to accomplish, some chitchat, a drink for them from Ben's bottle, and then on to the next home a mile or so farther along. We hoped that Ben would stay top-side-up as he joined each group and that the whisky would run out before we got to the tribes-folk in the interior. We didn't want him offering the tribesmen any. Incongruous combination: two missionaries who wanted to tell the tribespeople about the Lord, one bottle of whisky, and one Filipino guide who was getting happier and happier. Quite an evangelistic team! Fortunately, the bottle was spent before we got there. And, incidentally, so were we.

The journey seemed interminable. The delays and the constant rewetting of our shoes as we crossed the river time and again didn't help. Once the plains were behind us, we entered the river valley, with lushly covered mountains rising on either side, offering the beauty of all possible shades of green, highlighted with the silver of narrow waterfalls and little streams babbling their way to the river. But the river-bed itself was nothing but white or grey stones that reflected the glare and heat of the sun, the intensity defying the effectiveness of our sun glasses. The rocks varied from pebbles to solid slate. Some shifted under our feet, some we leaped on to, some we skirted, and some we dragged over. At high noon the sun beat on our heads, and our arms hung limp at our sides, our wet and soggy shoes leaving steaming trails on the sun-heated rocks as we clambered in and out of the water in our ascent. Rock, rocks and more rocks. Was there no end? We began to trip occasionally, then to stumble. We no longer saw the beautiful scenery, just the rocks, for every step had to be studied. I was ready to call it a day, except that heading home was more insane than going on. I was on the verge of tears. But Dode beat me to it. Wet eyes notwithstanding, she kept automatically putting one foot out in front of the other. I did likewise.

Ben encouraged us by telling us that the agreed place of rendezvous was just up the river a bit farther. We managed some enthusiasm—not, however, about finally meeting the Tadyawan, for weariness had sapped all evangelistic fervour. We just wanted to be able to take off our shoes and to stretch our toes, to slip into some dry, clean clothes, and to rest.

"There's the place," Ben called over his shoulder, pointing, for we were lagging considerably behind. "We have to cross only once more." We each sighed deeply and slowly. Could it really be? It was nearly supper-time, and we had started out early that morning!

"The path's difficult on the other side," he shouted above the noise of the water splashing over some huge rocks that made up part of a rocky cliff on the side he pointed to. "I hope you can make it," he said, obviously dubious. We hoped so too.

Ben led the way across the river, over a few more yards of rock, and then right up to the side of the high solid-rock cliff that stood perpendicular to the deep basin of water at its base.

"We'll have to find our footing along the face of the cliff," he said. "It's a short cut; otherwise we'd have to cut into the forest and climb up and over the mountain and come down on the other side." Too weary to do any more climbing than we had to, we agreed to try it. Feeling more secure in my bare feet, I hastily removed my shoes, tied them together by their laces, and threw them around my neck. I needed both hands for this venture, although what I thought I was going to hold on to I hadn't any idea. The rock-cliff had a broad, flat surface generally, but was just rough enough to afford little jagged places to put our feet

into as we edged over its surface. I clung to any little
jagged edge I could find. Two or three times my knees
buckled, but I caught myself each time, heart pounding at
the thought of falling down on to the huge rocks and then
slipping into the swirling water. At one point I had my
right foot in a tiny crevice where my left foot should have
been. It seemed impossible to advance and just as
impossible to retreat. Wet eyes again. How I prayed! And
then I was on the other side! All of us were. "Oh thank
you, dear Lord," was all I could say. Now we were
practically there at the chosen spot, the farm home of one
of the Filipino homesteaders and his family.

In the tall river grass leading up to the home we
changed into our dry clothes. They felt as clean and
comfortable as we had anticipated. At the steps of the
house we removed our shoes and made our way on to the
porch, then into the inner room that was filled with
brown bodies, some sitting on the bamboo floor, legs
outstretched, others huddled together to keep each
other's bare bodies warm as the night air settled in the
valley. Just the sight of all those tribespeople, about forty
of them, did wonders for our sagging spirits. I hadn't
thought anything would, or even could, earlier in the
day!

We made our way to a bare spot on the floor and sank
down, stealing glances at the fearful eyes that were also
stealing glances at us. Only Ben and the Filipino farmer
talked. The tribesmen, avoiding showing any kind of
emotion by their facial expressions, looked an unfriendly
group. Whenever my eye caught somebody surrep-
titiously studying me, his eyes hastily looked away. The
silence was unnerving. But then as I looked about the
room again, I noticed a familiar face with crossed eyes,
rotted teeth, and uncontrollably bushy hair. Why, it was

the man who carried the orchid to the sawmill that day about—was it really?—yes, about five years before! I was thrilled. I must have shown some signs of recognition, for he quickly said to Ben, "I know her." And what a wonderful reaction set in with that remark! His knowing me defrosted the entire atmosphere, and the tribesmen began to relax. They looked at us a little more openly and even asked a few questions about the things we tried to teach them. I spoke to them using a mixture of the Filipino language and the Tadyawan I had learned at Katubo's. Far from a good method, it was better than no method at all. We talked and taught on into the night, for, although earlier in the day while trekking we felt we would sleep the sleep of Rip van Winkle, sleep was overcome by delight.

When we all finally stretched out on the floor for the night's sleep, I told Dode all about the trip to the sawmill area five years before, how Hazel and I had been waiting for a logging truck to take us out to town, and how while we waited a little group of tribesmen had come along, an old man, a younger man, and two boys, one very sick with an ulcerated leg. I told her how they had listened to our records for only a short time and then left abruptly. "That little cross-eyed man was the younger of the two men in the little group that day," I explained. "Imagine, after not seeing him for five years!"

We wondered if something wonderful was going to come out of all this. Not knowing anything of the spirit-prophecy of a few decades previously, we had no idea that cross-eyed Pedro was also feeling that something good was ahead, for he was positive that we were the long-awaited strangers.

We closed our eyes to sleep. I saw nothing but rocks, but my heart was happily hopeful.

10 In a World of Demons

Many were the good visits we had with the Tadyawan in that Filipino home, but we began to be uneasy about the inconvenience we were causing the family. It was time for a change. We prayed much that the Lord would prepare the hearts of the Tadyawan for what we were going to suggest.

"We'd love to come and live with you right in your own homes," we proposed, trying to be casual. "We would learn your language from you, and then we could teach you the words of 'Our Father' from His Book."

Without any hesitation, Pedro, the spokesman in the absence of Bilbino, said, "That's what we want." *Oh, hallelujah!* we thought. Surely someday soon, some Tadyawan names were going to be written in the Lamb's Book of Life, for everything seemed to be dovetailing together. What did the five years' wait matter now?

And if we felt like shouting hallelujah then, we felt it many times after. Bilbino and all his household accepted us into their big family, treating us with kindness and thoughtfulness. They volunteered to carry our army packs on the trails so that we wouldn't get too tired on the hike (had they seen any of our tears?), and they got our drinking water for us to spare us the steep descent to the stream.

We accepted all their hospitality, eating whatever they cooked or half-cooked—anything from sweet potatoes to grubs—and sleeping on the floor beside them in their large, multi-family home, being awakened with them through the night by the crying babies or the sound of people chopping wood to build up the fire, when they were cold during the night. Not exactly like home, we thought, but we believed God was getting through to these Tadyawan.

At first we communicated through the Filipino language, but since neither they nor we felt at home in that language, we were eager to learn theirs, and they seemed just as eager that we learn it. Bilbino as the leader commanded someone to stay at home all day on each day of our short visits, just to teach us the Tadyawan language. Some made better teachers than others. "What's a *kosit?*" I asked Bilbino's eldest son, having heard the word in somebody's conversation. He looked at me with the most astounded expression, his mind apparently reasoning that if I already had the word, I surely must know what it is.

"A *kosit*," he repeated with all earnestness, "is a *kosit*." And then he gave his head a little jerk as if to say, "What else could a *kosit* be?" He'd never have won a teacher's certificate if *we* had to recommend him!

But not so Pedro. He would sit across from us on the floor by the hour patiently naming things and explaining anything that we wanted to know. Often his explanations were too full and far beyond our comprehension at that stage, but we kept saying "oh" to encourage him, and he kept right on. His spoken words far outnumbered what we wrote on our papers, and many times what we wrote was guesswork: things like, "He said this when I dropped my pencil through the floor down to the ground below. Maybe it means, What a pity! or Butterfingers! or Look out below!"

One day I asked Pedro, "What is a *makadet?*"

"Where did you hear that word?" he demanded in a surprisingly sharp tone.

"I guess I heard it last night while you were all talking," I defensively replied. "I don't know who said it. Is it your word?"

"Yes," he replied, and began to fidget with some pieces of rattan refuse that had been strewn about on the floor, stalling, not wanting to say any more.

"Well," I probed, "is it food or a tree or some kind of rock?"

"No." He sucked air through his front teeth. "It's like a person," he explained.

"What do you mean? Is it a real man like you?" I asked.

"No. It's a person of the night." The words rushed out of his mouth.

"A person of the night?" I repeated questioningly. "Well then, what are you?"

"I am a person of the day."

"Is this person of the night as tall as you?" I continued.

"No, it is very small," and with that he busied himself at the fireplace, obviously not wanting to pursue the matter further. I dropped the subject then, but not my curiosity. Just what and who was this person of the night?

A few days later I was checking all my material with Bilbino's oldest son again. I debated about asking him a definition for the word *makadet* lest I be meddling with tribal secrets, but then decided I would risk it.

"What's a *makadet*?" I asked casually.

His eyes shifted from my papers that always captured his interest and looked into space. He cupped his hands between his legs and squirmed uncomfortably.

"It's an animal," he said.

"Is it tame?"

"No, it bites people," and he scooted out of the house,

leaving me much confused by a definition so contradictory to Pedro's.

I later learned they were both right. Because the third person pronoun in Tadyawan is the same for both singular and plural, I had no idea at that time that I was talking about many *makadets* rather than merely one. But only after gathering little bits of information here and there, did I feel that I had the word for demon. They were legion, each with its own name, each with a different kind of body, and each one terrifying.

Even if we couldn't understand much of what they said about these demons, we could feel the fear they felt whenever we stumbled on to the subject. Lacking full understanding of the tenacious grip demons had on our forest people, we tried to get them to forget all about the demons and to trust in Our Father, who would keep them safely from all demon activity.

"Does that mean we won't get sick any more?" Bilbino inquired. We wondered about the connection between sickness and trusting in Our Father. But as the days went by, we gained more of their confidence, and they shared more of their tribal information with us. All sickness came from a demon. Each demon had his own particular brand. Demons bit people or struck them or walked over them while they slept, all of these actions resulting in sickness. Sometimes these demons caught a person's soul and imprisoned it. If that happened, the person became seriously ill. At other times the demons *ate* a person's soul, causing his death, no matter how many chants and offerings were made. "They wouldn't get well even if a man appealed to his wise-one," Pedro explained further.

"Who is this wise-one?" I inquired of him.

"He is a spirit that is more powerful than the demons; in fact, he can control the demons. Only a few people have a wise-one. If they do, they are given power to heal grave sicknesses or to release a person's soul from the demon-prison. They know how to divert curses, too, and they know when trouble is coming because their wise-one tells them. He also predicts the weather. To keep his wise-one making appearances to him, a man has only to obey all that the wise-one tells him to do."

"Do you have a wise-one?" I asked of Pedro.

"No, I have never even seen the demons, for even demons make appearances only to those they choose. Everybody, whether man or woman, wants to see the demons, but even though they perform the prescribed ceremony to be granted the power to see the demons, they don't necessarily see them."

I began making notes, while Pedro continued; "We have several rites a man can perform in seeking the power: He can hold burning sticks close to his eyes while he chants, or he can get a man with a wise-one to sprinkle his eyes with the juice of one of our vines, or he can request a smoke ceremony; but the demons don't always respond." I continued writing, and Pedro added, "Bilbino is the only one in our crowd who has a wise-one. That's why we regard him as our leader. He has knowledge now."

On another occasion we were all sitting in the home chewing on some sugar cane when one of the men came home from a jaunt across the river. "Golio is dead," he announced.

"His soul was eaten," joined in the others. "What a shame!"

"How could his soul be eaten?" I asked in complete ignorance. Nobody answered. Someone close to Bilbino mumbled something to him and he shuffled over the floor closer to us.

"The demons eat a man's soul while it roams around in the forest," he answered.

"But why does man's soul go off and leave him?" I asked, my curiosity mounting.

"Man's big soul always roams the forest. Only his little soul stays with him," he explained.

"How many souls does a man have?"

"Just the two."

"What happens to the little soul after the big one is eaten and the man dies?"

"The little soul leaves his left ear—that's where it always lives—and goes up to the stars; that is, if the man has been very good all his life. But that is very seldom. Most of the time his soul becomes an evil spirit, stalking the forest, satisfying its longing for company by causing the death of others among its former friends."

Demons, wise-ones, spirits of the dead; omens and taboos, chants and ceremonies, curses, divinations and communications with the spirits—was there no end to this involved system? We had read about animism in other parts of the world, with its witchdoctors, heathen dancers, and demon-possessed men who did phenomenal things. But we saw none of that in Tadyawan animism. There was no fanaticism, but rather a seemingly mild system whereby demons controlled fearful men and women, whose lives were spent in either trying to escape the demons altogether or in bargaining with them for some kind of peaceful co-existence.

As we taught them the Word of God, we could see that it was not their sin that held them back from accepting the Lord. It was this awful kingdom of darkness, mild in form but powerful, contrived by the Enemy himself. The whole system challenged the penetration of the gospel.

The Tadyawan liked to hear about Our Father, and

they obeyed the things they had learned from our teaching. They told us they would follow Him. But when we explained that they couldn't follow Our Father while they still had communication with the demons, they changed their minds. They hadn't meant to follow Him to the exclusion of the demons. It was too high a price to pay. The demons, they knew, would retaliate with sickness or death. Held tightly in the reality of the system, they could not break away. Our Father was less real to them than the demons. They had seen demons in bodily form; they had never seen Our Father. They had spoken with demons; they had never heard Our Father speak. We felt that somehow God was going to have to reveal Himself to them, showing them that He was alive and cared for them. We began to pray accordingly, asking the Lord to prove Himself to them in some miraculous way, whether in a dramatic manner or in a simple one. Not long after, God answered our prayer. It was a simple demonstration of His power, but it produced lasting results.

But first Our Father had to teach Dode and me something.

11 Demon Powers Weakened

Bilbino's oldest son, who loved to monopolize the conversation, was unusually quiet as he bent over the piece of paper he had borrowed from us. Pencil in hand, he very laboriously made marks on his paper. When he finished, he handed the paper to us and said, "See, I know how to write too."

We looked at the paper and saw a series of jiggly lines forming undefined shapes. "What does my writing say?" he quizzed us.

"Your words," and I elongated the vowels like they did when they were thinking, "are written nicely, but they do not say anything to me."

"Yes, they do," he insisted. "I wrote, 'Our Jesus takes away our sin'. See," and he pointed it out amidst the scribblings.

"Yes, good." I tried to be encouraging. "But when you write things, other people have to be able to read it. That's why everybody writes the same way. You'll have to write like everybody else does. Now watch. I'll tell you what I'm going to write, and then we'll ask my companion to read it to see if it is what I told you. I whispered the words, wrote them, then said to Dode, "Here, can you read this?"

Dode took the paper and read aloud from it exactly what I had whispered to him. His amazement knew no end. "I'd like to learn to write like that," he said eagerly.

"Someday we'll teach you, once we know your language better," we assured him.

The fraction of language that we had learned challenged us to progress as fast as we could, for they drank in all we could teach them from the Word of God. Bisi, Bilbino's youngest son, was helping me one day with a word that I had heard in conversation about a shrimp, but I still didn't understand its meaning. Bisi, struggling with shyness, finally got it across to me by a devious route.

"That means that the shrimp . . ." He spoke so fast I missed it again, leaving me looking as confused as I felt, which prompted him to add, "You know, like you said man does when he believes—he gets a new life and leaves the old one behind."

"Ah," and I wrote down "to shed skin." I had it at last!

"It's like that when a man dies too, isn't it?" Bisi asked. "He and his outer covering are separated. The outer covering goes up to heaven and the man himself stays here and soon rots."

"Oh, no," I contradicted. "That's backwards. Man's shell is his body. The real man is the part that goes to heaven. We will be real people in heaven, not just some kind of spirit. If you go to heaven, you'll know me when you see me, for I'll resemble me."

How excited the group became when they learned *that* truth! Heaven was becoming more attractive to them. Not only was it a good place, free from worry of starvation, but they would be more than anonymous spirits floating around in it—they would be real personalities, they would be themselves made new. That *was* good news!

Pitted against the drawing power of the Word, however, was the smirk of the demons, whose persuasive powers lay in their lifelong control of Tadyawan culture. This is the way their fathers lived, and their grandfathers, and their great-grandfathers, for as far back as anybody could remember. How could they completely forsake it?

"Don't mind if we make a racket tonight," Bilbino apologized one afternoon. "Later on we are going to kill a pig, and we'll be very noisy."

Then his wife sidled up to us, her old wrinkled face smiling deceptively. "We're going to give a pig to an ancestor's spirit tonight," she said, "but it's not real. We're doing it so that you can see how it's done."

"Yes," chimed in Pedro uneasily. "This is just for you to see how it's done."

We guessed otherwise.

We saw very little of that ceremony, however, for all the preparations were made beforehand away from the house. All we heard was Bilbino's son-in-law Marcos outside the house chanting in a monotone and then conversing.

"Did he see anything?" we asked after it was over and things were more normal again.

"Yes, he saw his mother's spirit. She was the one he wanted to contact."

So it was real! We were right. When, oh when, would they break away from all of that? In earnest we pleaded with the Lord to reveal Himself to them so that they would have the courage to break away.

Our visit there was finished for the time being, and we left for the plains where we had recently moved into a rough but homely little cottage in the quiet country several miles from the nearest town. After living in a one-room house with several tribal families, plus the dogs, cats, and pet monkeys constantly milling about, the stillness of our country cottage was just the relaxation and refreshment that we needed. In this cottage we analysed our language materials and prepared our teaching programme for the next trip in to the Tadyawan. Next door to our cottage was the home of a fine Filipino family of Christians. Theirs was the only house near us. Everywhere else was the rich green of the rolling plains, with clumps of coconut and banana plants growing beside small, thatch-roofed houses that dotted the plains in the foreground of our mountain view.

One day a young lad stood at our door, knocking lightly and calling, "*Tao po!* Somebody's here!" He was

selling a rooster, the only one he had and a nice looking
bird. Being located so far from the town we rarely had
access to fresh meat, so kept our larder stocked with
canned meat, which tested our culinary skills to the limit.
Relishing the thought of some fresh meat for dinner, we
decided to take the bird; not even the inevitable
toughness deterred us. We bought it for about fifty cents
and tied it up to a pole of the house, out by the kitchen
steps. Then we went about our language work with
visions of fresh chicken intruding into problems with verb
affixation and sentence structure.

Typing vigorously, we hardly heard Granny Cruz from
next door calling us, "Somebody's here!" She persisted,
however, and soon was telling us the sad story that our
chicken had escaped. She had been in her yard and saw it
just as it detached itself from our poorly-tied string and
took off across the yard and out into the fields. She was
sympathetic. "All that money wasted! It just isn't right.
Somebody else will get the chicken you paid for. We must
pray," she said as she left, "and ask the Lord to bring the
chicken back to you."

Our "yes" to that suggestion was a bit weak. Neither of
us had ever prayed for a chicken before; and if the truth
were told, we weren't sure how we felt about praying for
it, nor did we really care very much that it had gone. To
have fresh meat would have been nice, but it was no
tragedy not to have it. We were a bit relieved, in fact, to
realize that we were spared the slaughtering of it—an
undertaking worthy of note, we being females—and
could resort to the customary cans that required no
cleaning or dressing. Dinner, corned beef, was on our
platters in no time. We returned thanks and, because
sweet Granny had suggested it, we casually mentioned the
chicken to the Lord, telling Him to bring it back if He
thought we should have it.

And sure enough, when dusk was deepening the many shades of green that made up our panoramic view of the mountains, the time when people settle down and chickens begin to roost, Dode bounced into my room and yelled, "Hey, the chicken's back! It's just roosted in the tree outside the bedroom window."

"Let's get it straight away," I said with a laugh. But Dode knew a bit more about chickens than I did.

"No, let's leave it there for now. It won't come down," she assured me, "till morning."

I was reluctant to agree, feeling that we'd better not test the Lord further, but grab the wandering fowl right away. However, Dode was so positive that I acquiesced; and sure enough, the first sound that woke me while it was still dark next morning was Dode crawling out from under her mosquito net and stealthily opening and passing through the door and out to the tree. And then everything happened at once: lots of squawk, flutter, flap, and more squawk and above it all Dode's triumphant shout, "I've got it!" Then things were still, and in the stillness a sweet little voice drifted from the bedroom next door into our bedroom window: "Praise the Lord!" Granny had heard the catch too. In simple faith she had claimed and received, and then praised.

At mid-morning the beast took quite a ceremonious slaughtering, for our knife was dull. But the chicken was soon sizzling in our little portable oven, and at dinner we enjoyed its crispy crunch and roasted flavour. Mealtime was longer than usual, however, for it took a lot of chewing. In less than no time, though, we forgot all about that incident, never considering that it held any significance for us.

Several days later, when our Tadyawan Bible lessons were all prepared and the flannelgraph cut out, we were ready for another trip into the Banos mountains to be with Pedro and the Tadyawan there. We jammed our army packs full of the things we would need for the trip—dried fruit, canned meat, two changes of clothing and our language materials. Then we closed up the cottage, leaving it to the inevitable invasion of field mice and rats, and dashed down our path to catch the bus we could hear coming along our country road. The dull, cloudy morning climaxed the few days of on-and-off torrential rains we had had.

Arriving at the Banos River, we were disappointed to find it in spate, defying our crossing. If we couldn't make this first crossing, we knew the Tadyawan would never have ventured down the mountains to meet us, for they had to make about thirty-one other crossings to get to our place of rendezvous and then lead us back to their homes the same way they had come. However, having once closed our cottage, with everything packed in trunks or cupboards away from the destructive rodents (whose favourite chew, incidentally, was Tupperware), we were in no mood to return, to open the cottage again, unpack all the equipment and set up housekeeping for the few days the river needed to resume a lower water level. So we decided to make a trip up to the northern part of the island to visit some of the Tadyawan on the Aglobang River. We had been teaching them somewhat spasmodically in between some of our trips to the Tadyawan at the Banos, and their interest egged us on to continued visits. We hoped that it hadn't rained up there and that the river would be crossable. It was. We travelled along its banks, or through its waters when banks became steep rock walls. Then leaving the river, we took to a mountain trail. Suddenly in the thick of the forest we met one of the Tadyawan men who had shown interest in the Word of God, but who was still very much afraid of us.

He never hung around us for very long, and he was always adamant in his refusal to pose for our camera, even after others had overcome their fears. This day, however, his face lit up when he saw us. "Oh," he said, "I knew you were coming today."

We were taken aback. How did he know? We hardly knew ourselves, and surely nobody else knew. "How did you know we were coming?" I asked.

"I saw Jesus last night, and He told me you would be here today," he explained, wrinkling up his nose and fidgeting like he always did, looking as if he was in a hurry to proceed on his journey in the opposite direction from us. We didn't try to detain him. But his tale? Had he seen the Lord? If so, why didn't the Lord tell him to listen to the teaching of the Word? Or had he seen a demon impersonating one of the pictures of Christ that we had shown him during a Bible story lesson on some previous visit? We were powerfully persuaded that the Tadyawan world was not one of imaginary ghosts and phantoms, but one of direct contact with the very kingdom of darkness; not merely a casual acknowledgment of the existence of these demons, but a life of complete bondage under their influence.

After a few days spent in the Aglobang area, we struck out for the south again, only to get to the Banos to find it still impassable. Was this some trick of the enemy to keep the Tadyawan from growing in their knowledge and understanding of God's Word? We feared what big gaps between our visits to them could mean. The last time we had been with them, they told us of the death curse the Tawbuid tribesmen in the interior had put on all of them because they had welcomed us into the mountains. Outsiders like us were taboo. The Tawbuid didn't want us so close to their homes, disturbing their traditions and

practices, lest it incur the wrath of the demons and thus
bring evil on their own heads, so they intended to keep us
out. The curse was the only method they knew to prevent
danger to themselves. It would mean death for all of the
Tadyawan, and the Tadyawan were terrified. We had
promised to pray for them all, but our delay in getting
back to them would leave them very vulnerable. Our faith
wavered at the thought. Could they stand up under such a
temptation? They knew so very little of the mightiness of
our God.

We slid our packs off our backs and dropped them on
to the ground, then sat on a damp log to have some
prayer and to enjoy a bite to eat from our packed picnic
lunch. As we ate, along came the epitome of darkness.
We had seen the man before, a tall, dirty-skinned
Tawbuid, another pipe smoker. He had visited Bilbino's
household a few times while we were there. He would
have walked right past us had we not stopped him to ask
if he had seen any of the Tadyawan along the way. He
hadn't. Did he think they were home? Yes. With that, we
asked him if he would help us through all the river
crossings so that we could get into their area. We had
forgotten for the moment that he was a Tawbuid and
probably one of the group who was compelled to go
along with cursing us. But, nicely enough, in the
emergency he either forgot or overlooked the fact too, for
he agreed to take us in. "But I won't be going that
direction until tomorrow," he added. That meant not
only delay, but our going all the way back to our lowland
cottage for the night; yet we had a guide for the trip into
the mountains and took comfort from this fact.

The next day we met our guide, looking just as
fearsome as he had the day before. Together we headed
inland. At each river crossing, he thoughtfully took us by

the hand and guided us across the muddy, turbulent Banos, feeling for safe footing with his walking-stick. The swollen river hindering our hurrying, the day was a long and weary one.

Late in the afternoon we emerged into the clearing of our Tadyawan home, only to find the house deserted. Not even a stray chicken scratched around the edge of the forest for morsels. Again our faith faltered. We reasoned that the curse had been too much for our friends, and they had fled in fear, not wanting to hear the gospel any more. It was the situation we had faced at Katubo's area all over again.

Our guide suggested that we stay in the abandoned house for the night and wait to see if anybody showed up in the morning. We did, but having left our bedding in the custody of the vanished Tadyawan, we shivered sleepless through the cold night. In the morning, stiff and chilled to the bone, we sat dejectedly in the house waiting for the sun's rays to warm us up and to burn off the dew, not daring to hope that the miserable night had been worth while. Suddenly, however, we heard voices outside. And there stood Pedro and two others! How glad we were to see them! They seemed glad to see us too, much surprised that we had successfully managed to cross the flood waters.

How faithless we had been! Not only did they take us to their new home, but we found them their usual friendly, warm selves; and they were still very interested in the Word of God.

The enemy hadn't won after all! How grateful we were that the One who said, "According to your faith be it unto you," also caused it to be written, "Though we believe not, yet He abideth faithful"!

After we had been there two days, they approached us

seriously one morning, "You have been teaching us that Our Father says that whatever we ask He will do. Now, you pray to Our Father to bring our pig back."

"Where is your pig?" we asked, only half believing our ears.

"We don't know. It ran away."

"How long ago?"

"Three days," came back the unwelcome reply.

Three days? In thick forest? We fairly groaned within. That pig could have been quite far away by that time, and very much lost. And yet . . . Our thoughts raced quickly. Had God been preparing us for this moment? If He could bring back our runaway chicken in response to Granny's faith, why not a pig? We needed no further guidance.

"All right," we said, "let's all gather together and ask Our Father as a family to bring the pig back home again." A real scramble followed as all the folk—men in G-strings, scantily rag-covered women and naked children—crouched and clambered back into the house, covering the floor and blocking the doorway.

When all had bowed their heads and closed their eyes—though the scuffling continued—we offered our request to Our Father. With that the folk went on their ways, some to the fields to weed around the rice plants, some to the stream to see what they could catch in the way of a fish treat. We went on with our language study.

That day passed quickly, and also the night. The following morning Dode and I were inside the house with some of the children. All the others had left for the outside chores. The low, broad doorway in the house gave us a good view of the outside grounds and the forest that rimmed the clearing, including the path that led up to the house. As we chatted, along came Piping, with face expressionless, but eyes fairly gleaming. He was carrying a pig on his shoulder. Without saying a word, he approached the house and shrugged the pig off his shoulder on to the house floor, which was shoulder height. So engrossed was I and so undemonstrative his performance that I hardly took notice of him. Dode, however, stared and then burst out, "Hey, do you think that could be the pig we prayed for?"

We asked him. "Yes," he replied, smiling the victor's smile.

"Well then, let's call everybody together again so that we can thank Our Father for answering our prayer." Everybody gathered in much the same fashion as they had the day before, but now they were quite jubilant.

That night, we heard a slaughtering. It was the pig, the one we had prayed for, and everyone enjoyed a good pork supper with rice. To us it was a shame to kill a monument to answered prayer so quickly. "Why did you kill the pig?" we asked at an appropriate moment.

They replied innocently, "Oh, it might have run away again." *How human!* we thought as we chuckled to each other. They could trust Our Father to bring the roaming pig back, but they couldn't trust Him any longer to keep it there!

The next day when we all gathered around the fireplace for some Bible study, prayer and singing, the people seemed restless and excited about something. We couldn't understand what it was all about, but we could feel it in the very atmosphere. We started to teach them a Bible story, when Pedro interrupted us.

"We have something to say to you."

"Go ahead," we encouraged.

"We have all decided that today, right now, we want to pray to Our Father and ask Him to take away our sin."

Hallelujah! He had answered our prayer! The Lord had revealed Himself to them in a language that they knew, and now they were wanting to come to Him. The prayer was simple and short, and while we knew that that didn't automatically make them all Christians, we felt sure that some had made real transactions with God that day.

On our very next visit to them they had another prayer request, this time it was for fish. "We're going to dam off part of the river to catch some fish; so will you pray to Our Father and ask Him to give us lots of fish?" We were tempted to give them a sermon on not always asking for things, but then thought better of it. After all, maybe the Lord wanted to confirm His interest in them. As a community, then, we prayed again, and they went off to their fishing quite elated with confidence. Their faith was rewarded. Back they came laden with fish, all sizes and kinds. We all had fish for supper that night, then for breakfast the next day, and for lunch and for supper; it went on into the third and fourth day. Our noses guided us to turn down their offers after the second day, what with no refrigeration! "It would give us tummy-ache now if we ate it when it smells bad like that," we explained. But they were completely bewildered.

"It gives us tummy-ache too," they replied, "but so what? We like fish, so we just go ahead and eat it anyway, even if it does smell."

They listened more intently to the Word after that, elated to think that now they had found someone interested in them to give them good things. They had found the touchstone to prosperity. We weren't worried. Someone has said about the animistic tribesman that "he marched into the Christian camp of freedom, never dreaming of the long, weary warfare awaiting him". We had confidence that the Lord knew how to balance the thinking of His children and how to challenge them to engage in the fight against the enemy and to dare to walk closely and exclusively with Himself.

12 A Vision Brings the Tawbuid

Outside, the forest was dripping from shivering leaves. Inside, it was cozy and cheerful, the kind of evening when everybody liked everything and everybody. The cat sat hunched on one of the logs in the fireplace napping contentedly in the warmth of the little glow, occasionally shifting position and throwing grotesque shadows on the wall, disturbing the peacefulness of vivid imaginations. One by one the household stretched themselves out on the floor, here a lump under a dirty brown blanket, there another, and then several lumps all huddled together as mother and children tried to keep each other warm. This was the kind of night we loved when we were with the Tadyawan, and we too curled up under our flannel blanket, heads propped on our plastic bags of clothing, listening to the cheerful conversation. We couldn't understand all that they said, but we caught the mood and were cheerful along with them. Then suddenly, someone called over to us, "What is *baboy* in your language?"

"Here we go again," we sighed, poking each other in the ribs, for we knew this was the beginning of a lengthy English lesson. We took turns in the answers.

"Pig," we replied in answer to his question.

"Pig?" they repeated questioningly, checking on their pronunciation.

"Yes, pig."

"*Balay*," pounced a voice from a far corner.

"House," we interpreted.

"Ouse?"

"Not really; it's *h*ouse!" and we emphasized the "h"—a sound foreign to them. Their efforts to produce it were hilarious. Wives laughed hysterically at their husbands' attempts as they moved their heads forward to help the "h" come out in exaggerated puffs of air. It was fun for us all. But the list lengthened; they questioned, we answered, they repeated; we corrected, then said the word again, and they mimicked again on into the night.

"Your language is very hard," spoke up Pedro, who lay beside his fireplace chewing on a piece of rattan that was sticking out of his mouth. "I think it will take us ten years to learn each other's languages. But maybe you'll get tired of coming by that time."

We assured him that we wouldn't, and from those who were still awake came all kinds of grunts of satisfaction. Then Pedro asked further, "Will we know all of Our Father's words by that time?"

"I don't think so," I replied. "My companion and I have been studying His papers for a long time, maybe twenty years, and we still don't know it all; nor do we understand it all. That's why we're always reading it."

That was an overwhelming thought to them, and there was a very long pause. Then Bilbino spoke up, "Does everybody in your country read His papers?"

"No, not everybody, because not everybody believes in Him." They were staggered by this admission and chatted among themselves for a while.

"Are all the people in your country going to bed now

like we are?" We admired their zest for learning whatever we could teach them, but we were getting sleepy.

"No," we explained. "It's daytime over there now." If any of those who hadn't yet gone to sleep were feeling the pull of their wooden pillow, they felt the pull no longer. They were wide awake with this news. It called for lots of explanation from us, the travels of the earth and the moon, the position of the sun, the shape of the earth.

"If the earth moves," giggled Bilbino behind his short-fingered hand, "why aren't we dizzy? And if it is round, like you say, why don't some people fall off the bottom?"

We were getting into language difficulties and had to promise a better explanation when we learned more of their language. Bilbino, however, had lots of puzzling thoughts that he still wanted to know the answers to.

"How can the earth move around when it stands on those eight big poles that our grandfathers have told us about?" he asked.

"Oh, but the earth doesn't stand on poles at all. It's just a round ball in the heavens," we corrected.

"No, we'll all fall!" he screeched, and everybody agreed.

"Oh no," we said, "Our Father holds the earth in His hand. He made the earth, and He knows how to keep it right where it is in the heavens. He takes care of the whole earth."

"But how can He? While He is looking after the people on the top of the ball, who looks after the people underneath?"

"Our Father does."

They laughed and then yelled in all good humour, giving us their usual retort to something incredible: "That's a lie."

"But no," we said, "you see, Our Father is not like

man. Man can only be in one place at a time, but Our Father is everywhere. He looks after His people here on your island and at the same time looks after the people who believe in Him on the other islands."

It was too much for them to comprehend and gave them much to think about. Soon the chatting died down, and we all buried ourselves further into our blankets and went to sleep.

The next day a group of Tawbuid tribesmen arrived at the house, big men, most of them with skin scruffy from ringworm, but all silent, sober and observant. Our Tadyawan women looked afraid; our men warily alert. Eventually, however, they exchanged a sentence or two, gradually leading into a real conversation. As the two groups talked, we handed the Two Roads poster to some of the Tadyawan sitting on the outside of the circle and said encouragingly, "It would be nice if you would teach the Tawbuid something about Our Father before they left."

They quickly objected, "We don't know enough of Our Father's words yet."

But we urged them. "These Tawbuid will go to the big fire if they don't believe, and how will they believe if somebody doesn't tell them what Our Father says in His papers? We'd teach them, but we don't know their language. Since most of you men know their language, it's really up to you. Teach them as much as you know."

All their fidgeting and looking about revealed the effort it was for them to dare such a thing, but finally one of the men plunged into the subject. Holding the poster in his own two hands so that he could see it, he tried to relate what it was all about. He mimicked us perfectly. At one point he grabbed our New Testament, opened it, flipped its pages, and pointed to some of its verses to confirm what he was saying. He had no idea what he was pointing to, and we had no idea what he was saying, but we enjoyed his earnest attempt. Bilbino, never one to be outdone in these things, started his own little preaching campaign, but we could tell from his arm and hand gestures that his topic was the shape and movement of the earth. They all laughed uproariously at what he taught. The visit that started out so forebodingly ended very happily. After the Tawbuid left, we suggested that the Tadyawan teach all their visitors, even when we were not there with them, so that all their neighbouring tribesmen would hear the words of Our Father, whether the neighbours were Tadyawan or Tawbuid.

"Down south here, there are very few Tadyawan," someone said. "But there are lots of Tawbuid."

On a subsequent visit they had a surprise for us—a new house that they had built down beside the Banos River, away from the immediate Tadyawan community, but accessible to them as well as to the Tawbuid. "We built this house so that you would see some Tawbuid when you come to visit us; then you can teach them too, for this is the way the Tawbuid travel, along the rivers." We liked the Tadyawan initiative. And they were right. We saw lots of Tawbuid in that area. They'd drop in to have a chat with some of the Tadyawan and always got something about the Word from us through our Tadyawan who knew their language. Some of the Tawbuid were too fearful of us to come back after the first visit, but others of them came again and again, losing their fears. We found them gentle, fun-loving, and eager to hear the Word of God.

Sadly enough, the best Tawbuid speaker we had was Bilbino and, as leader of the group, he assumed his rightful role. But he was showing unhealthy signs in his attitude toward the Word, and often we wished that he would step into the background and let Pedro or Mabilis do the teaching, for those two were sincerely responding to all the teaching we gave them. But, as Paul said, whether in pretence or in truth, the gospel was preached, and the Tawbuid were showing signs of real interest. It baffled us a little, for a couple of our fellow-missionaries, the Russell Reeds, had been trying to gain an opening into this tribe for several years, but no break seemed to come. Was the opening going to come here?

One day I was talking with Pedro about the Tawbuid and their interest in the Word of God, saying that it was something we had been praying about for a long time, but that the Tawbuid had always remained aloof to us missionaries and our teaching.

"Do you know why they're coming?" Pedro asked me.

I hadn't any idea apart from the Lord's answering prayer. "No," I confessed, "I don't really know. But lots of people have been praying and so have you."

"Yes," said Pedro, "but besides that, see that man over there?" He pointed to a big Tawbuid, lighter in colour than some of the others because he was a ringworm victim. His huge eyes had a perpetual look of surprise. His name was Tiban.

"A long time ago," Pedro continued, "Tiban's father had a dream that strangers were going to come to our island and bring good teaching. His father told Tiban to be sure to follow the good teaching when the strangers came. And that's why he's coming now. He's the leader of all that group of eight families; so they all come with him. He thinks maybe you women are the ones that his father spoke about."

Not yet knowing the story of Aplaki, I found Pedro's explanation most interesting. Had the Lord prepared the way for the Tawbuid to hear the Word even before we ever got to them? Pedro went on speaking: "You know, that's why we listened to you too and asked you to come. A friend of Bilbino's saw a vision many years ago, even before my wife was born. From what you have taught us it must have been an angel of Our Father. The angel told him to pass the word along to the others that some day you would come. We were all waiting for you. That's why we weren't afraid of you when we saw you."

I talked to some of the others about it and plied Bilbino with questions. Gradually the story of Aplaki's vision unfolded, leaving us missionaries awed and praiseful. To the animistic tribesmen, dreams and visions and omens were the language of another world, but a world they understood. God had spoken in their language. They understood and responded.

13 The Curse

"The Tawbuid are really interested in Our Father's words," Mabilis told us one day. He was sitting on the riverbank atop a huge rock, splitting some rattan that he had just cut down from the forest trees. A few yards away the Banos River dashed noisily toward the sea, splashing over the rocks, and carrying with it right at that moment some Tadyawan, screaming with glee. They were riding astride an old tree trunk, travelling at great speed in the current, and turning this way and that, depending on the way the rocks in the riverbed were arranged. The more the trunk swirled, the louder their screams and the funnier their antics. Running alongside on the river's edge, hopping over rock after rock, other Tadyawan and Tawbuid cheered the riders on.

"But they're not really believing yet," continued Mabilis. "They say they're still testing your words to see if they're good." More shouts of laughter came from the river's edge. Pedro's wife had just fallen into the water.

"Well, you men will have to keep telling them the things that we teach you so that they'll understand and begin to obey Our Father," we said, letting our gaze wander toward the river. The log riders were pretty far downstream by that time and one by one they were purposely throwing themselves into the water to halt their ride, knowing it would be a long walk back otherwise.

"You and the Tawbuid seem to be getting along quite well with each other," we observed.

"Yes, we're friends now," and Mabilis smiled a reminiscent kind of smile, perhaps recalling the first days when they were all wary and suspicious of each other.

"We noticed that they're bringing their wives and children along too. That must mean that they're not afraid of us either, any more."

"No, they're not afraid of you now," he assured me and Dot Reiber, who was then working with me in the absence of Dode. "And they say they want to hear much more of Our Father's words."

Their desire, however, didn't stand uncontested for long. Does the devil ever let anything go unchallenged? Several of us were sitting chatting in the small house by the river, when Bilbino's eldest daughter, who was Mabilis's mother, came running up the path that led to the house, all the paraphernalia on her necklace jingling or clacking as she ran. It was obvious that she brought important tidings. She hopped on to the pole step of the house and breathlessly shouted to us in a high-pitched voice, "Don't drink any more water from that little stream near the house. We have just learned that the Tawbuid in the interior are mad at all of us and they've blown smoke." (It was the Tawbuid expression for putting a death curse on people.) Catching a deep breath, she repeated it again, "They've blown smoke on us all—you, us Tadyawan, and the Tawbuid that are coming to listen to the teaching. They've caused the curse to travel down the very stream where you two sisters get your water; so don't ever draw any water from there again. Go to the Banos to get your water from now on."

The intensity of her fear was immediately contagious. No one moved, but their eyes bespoke their great terror. The whole community was cursed! Sickness and sure death for all of them! They knew that curses, regardless of their content, were effective. A curse was no mere threat. The ways of demons were deadly, and these folk knew it. They had proof in their own clan: Doling had been cursed so that all of her girl babies were to die. She had lost all three of her little girls. Manindok had also been cursed so that none of his children would grow up. One by one he had lost nine children. And Foltito's wife had been cursed into sterility. She had never had any children.

In their silence, Dot and I sat silent too. Was this an opportunity to prove God before the eyes of the Tawbuid as well? Someone turned to us and repeated calmly what Bilbino's daughter had said earlier, "You'd better not drink out of the stream any more."

"But we're not afraid of that curse," we astounded them by saying. "You see, we belong to Our Father, and He's stronger than the demons that help the enemy Tawbuid. He will take care of us. We're going to ask Him to protect us, and we're going to drink that water anyway. He'll not let anything harm us."

Pedro turned toward us, his face searching as his thoughts circled the circumference of our idea; and then suddenly the light of the discoverer came into his eyes. "Yes, that's right," he announced with conviction, "that's what we should all do—pray to Our Father and ask Him to protect us." He punctuated his statement with a firm nod of his head. In the days and weeks that followed, we all laid hold of the Lord for His protection. Pedro's confidence inspired confidence in the others, and as we prayed earnestly for protection the Lord removed their fear.

Pedro's faith was growing, and right along with him was Mabilis. They were pals, even though Pedro was a married man with a family and was almost twice as old as single Mabilis. These two seriously took on the task of teaching the Tawbuid when they came to live with us and the Tadyawan for several days at a time. These visitors' keen interest now outmatched Bilbino's limited understanding.

Mabilis and Pedro were patient and persuasive, and the Tawbuid responded, wanting to follow the Lord, though understanding very little of the cost involved. Thus far, in their minds they were dealing with a good spirit who wanted to help them rather than with the demons whose help they had to induce. When they saw the Tadyawan returning thanks before they ate their sweet potatoes or rice, the Tawbuid returned thanks too. When they noticed the Tadyawan prayed before they left the house for work in the fields, the Tawbuid followed that pattern too. On one of the first occasions, three Tawbuid men crouched in the doorway of the house, knives in their sheaths all ready for a day of felling trees. After lots of whispering and tittering they bowed their heads and prayed audibly. Usually the Tadyawan prayer was brief, but these

Tawbuid prayed on and on. Being within earshot, we stopped talking to listen and heard them repeating over and over again the same few sentences. Pedro and Mabilis were also nearby and heard what we had heard. They exchanged smiles and a few hurried words, then shuffled over beside the Tawbuid trio, who were still praying with heads bowed. Mabilis waited for the one praying to take a breath, then he quickly cut in and finished the prayer with a sentence and an "Amen." The Tawbuid hurried off to their work, while Mabilis and Pedro chuckled together. "They couldn't stop praying," they explained to us, "because they had forgotten how to end their prayer."

Thus, curse or no curse, the Tawbuid, encouraged by the boldness of the Tadyawan, refused to be deterred. They continued to come for the teaching, even though they were getting only the spiritual crumbs that fell from the Tadyawan table, which itself bore only crumbs from us because we hadn't enough yet of the Tadyawan language to do any extensive teaching. The Tawbuid always gave good attention to what was being taught to them, but one day they seemed restless and unsettled as they sat on the floor while Mabilis taught what Pedro prompted him to say. They chatted among themselves, or dug into their tobacco pouches or reached for roasted potatoes stored in the palm-leaf roof. It was hard going for Mabilis, disturbed by their inattention, for he earnestly wanted them to understand and believe.

But if he was feeling frustrated, it didn't show in his tone of voice as he seriously appealed to them, "Say, you fellows, you should listen to what we're teaching you. These are Our Father's words, not ours. It's Our Father who's telling you these things. We are just His middlemen."

Middlemen of God! If only it were true of more of the

Tadyawan there! Even though the whole group had prayed with us that day after the pig was found, it seemed as if only Pedro and Mabilis were going on step by step, haltingly, but going on. We really wondered about the others.

Timid and puzzled, Pedro approached us privately one day. "Ever since you taught us that we can't believe in Our Father if we don't stop listening to the demons, Bilbino has lost interest. He told us he wouldn't forbid us to listen if we wanted to, but he said he would believe in his own way, following the demons as well."

This was disturbing news, although not altogether unexpected. Our suspicions had been aroused some weeks previously when we missed him one Sunday and asked, "Where's Bilbino? Isn't he coming to the service today?"

His wife, blind now in one eye and going deaf, unthinkingly answered, "No, his wise-one told him not to come today; so he stayed home." Funny little lovable woman, she was too dull herself to comprehend any of the teaching, but she was our friend. She liked to mother us and had a very commanding way of bossing people into doing what she thought we needed. So alert to our needs. So unaware of her own.

"What does Our Father say about marriage?" she asked us one day, patting her head as she talked, to relieve some of the itching. No doubt marriage was a current subject with the Tadyawan because by the time we grabbed our Bibles and opened the pages, a group of them had gathered around us.

"A very important thing He tells us is that believers should marry only believers."

"Does He let us marry close relatives?" Dolilaw asked.

"No, He forbids that. He has written that we are not to marry our brothers or sisters, or our aunts or uncles."

"Just like our grandfathers taught us," they interrupted with great satisfaction.

"Can a man have two wives?" Bilbino inquired.

"No, Our Father says that a husband and wife are really one, and they are to love and care for each other as long as they live."

"Oh!" It was a new thought to them, for there were Tadyawan in other areas who had two or more wives. Bilbino pondered that for a moment, and then said, "But in our culture, it's all right. A man can have two wives."

"Yes," agreed his wrinkled little wife. "If a man's wise-one tells him he can have another wife, nobody objects to it. The only restriction is that there's to be no fighting in the home once the second wife is brought in." Her voice sounded slyly persuasive. We wondered about it, but not for long.

"Does everybody Our Father talks about in His papers have names?" Bilbino asked one day as he sat cutting his toenails with his long jungle knife.

"We guess they did," we replied, "although He doesn't always mention what their names were."

"Well, then, will you hunt in His papers for a name for my wife? She has never had a name."

"What kind of a name would she like?"

"I don't know," he replied.

"You told us some time ago that she is getting old and can no longer bear children. Is that right?" we asked, already inspired.

When he grunted a yes, we suggested the name "Sala", which is Tadyawan for Sarah, and hoped that he wouldn't press the Lord for a perfect analogy. "She was the wife of Abraham and was too old to have children, remember?" we jogged his memory. "That name would suit your wife." He liked it and shouted her name across to her. Then he moved even closer to us and in low, confidential tones said, "That's why I would like another wife. We Tadyawan like large families and since my wife can't have children any more, I would like to marry a younger woman who can."

"But if you're really believing like you claim to be, then you can't," we objected. "It would be disobedient to Our Father. When a man has a wife, she is his wife forever. Only death separates them. He cannot send her away and take another wife."

"Oh, but you don't understand. I wouldn't send my wife away. She'd live with me still and be my wife. But I would have two wives. According to us, that's all right as long as we don't fight."

"But Our Father doesn't approve," we insisted.

In the next weeks, repeated conversations with Bilbino brought the same question to the fore, "Does Our Father consider it wrong for me to take a second wife?" Our plain, persistent "yes" was no match for his adamant will, and we tired of repeating it when he looked and talked so unyieldingly.

"Does He consider it wrong if I take another wife?" he asked once again when nobody was around except Dode, who had returned to the Tadyawan, and me. We were exasperated, and our "yes" flew at him out of impatience.

"But I saw Jesus in a dream last night, and He told me I could have a second wife," he asserted sincerely, trying to prove that he was being guided aright in his decision.

We were stunned. There it was again. A dream—a vision of Jesus. But it wasn't hard to determine the source of that vision. "That wasn't Jesus you saw last night," we quickly corrected. "It was a demon impersonating Jesus so that you would be fooled into doing the wrong thing. Even the devil has power to turn himself into something beautiful just to trick people No, that was undoubtedly a demon, for Jesus wouldn't say something to you contrary to what Our Father has written in His papers."

He remained unconvinced; so did his wife, now called Sala by everyone. "Let him have another wife," she implored of us one day, evidently fearing he would run off and leave her altogether and marry someone else. Little did she know the heartache that awaited her, for he pursued his wilful way and eventually married the pretty little sister of his son-in-law Marcos. Though she was still a child of about fourteen years when he married her, her attitudes were those of an older woman. She wanted no rival. In her exceeding jealousy she rebelled against any attention that Bilbino gave to Sala. From then on, there was continual fighting and bickering in that house, and all the Tadyawan became upset over it.

"I wish you'd talk to my father," Pedro's wife said to us after we had arrived in the mountains for another month's visit. "We tell him how awful it is to fight like that, but he won't listen to us."

"But he won't listen to us either," we assured her. "We told him not to take another wife in the first place, but it didn't stop him. Why do you think he'll listen to us now?"

"He'll listen," she insisted. "Just talk to him."

We waited for an opportunity, wondering what we would say and how we should say it. Bilbino himself gave us the opportunity we wanted. He rushed up the pole step and into the house one rainy afternoon and sat beside us on the floor, half shyly approaching his problem by indirectly asking a question: "Does Our Father object to fighting in the home?"

"Yes, it isn't right to quarrel," we admonished him.

"Well, then," he proclaimed, "Sala has got to leave our home. If quarrelling is wrong to Our Father, I can't have it continue. Sala will have to go." Dode and I were shocked into silence by his selfish unreasonableness.

A broken-hearted and lonely Sala left his house, living alternately with her children and their families. The separation from Bilbino was hard to take, for she had loved him very much. Their animistic world was cold and cruel. She found no comfort anywhere.

How far back now would Bilbino go? we wondered. How far had he come? We didn't know. But because Bilbino was now the established leader of the group, and groups always followed their leader's preferences, we wondered who would follow Bilbino back into the darkness that disobedience leads to. We feared for Pedro's wife. She had great respect for her father and had always followed his advice. If she went back to the old demon ways, what would happen to the emerging faith of Pedro? We trembled for him, for he was devoted to his strong-willed wife, who had inherited her father's humour and her mother's industry. One little remark of his, however, gave us great hope. "Is it all right for a man to believe even if his wife doesn't want to?" he asked us one day. We knew he meant himself. We felt he was saying, "I want to follow the Lord, but my wife doesn't. Will Our Father accept me anyway?"

We felt it was time to lay living stones on the foundation laid for the Tadyawan church. One Sunday morning during our Bible study together we taught about baptism, its importance and its significance, ending up the lesson with, "If you know that you have left the old life and have had your sins washed away by the blood of Jesus Christ and in your heart you desire to follow the Lord, then you can be baptized. If any of you would like to be, you can let us know." We had no idea who would respond to the suggestion, but we hoped Pedro and

Mabilis would, for they showed signs of a new life within. Several days later Dolilaw came to us, saying, "Most of us do not feel ready for baptism, but if anybody should be baptized, it should be Pedro and Mabilis. They are really following all that Our Father says." And sure enough, a few days later Pedro and Mabilis together came and said that they wanted to be baptized because they wanted to walk on Our Father's path all of their lives.

Baptism day came, with everybody, including the Tawbuid, excited over this new adventure. We had invited Russell Reed to perform the baptism ceremony, and he alone remained calm. In a little rivulet of the Banos River he baptized the two young men, but Pedro and Mabilis were both so nervous that their voices were barely audible as they publicly answered the questions Russ asked them about their salvation and new life in Christ. Mabilis's body shook visibly under the gaze of the whole Tadyawan and Tawbuid community, causing a few titters from the crowd.

After their baptism we five went back to the house and ate the Lord's Supper together, again under the gaze of every attentive eye. Eating a previously roasted sweet potato and drinking sugar cane juice out of a tiny bamboo cup that Pedro had made, we gave thanks for the Lord's broken body and shed blood, glad together that we were now one family in Christ. It was a happy day, the beginning of what we had hoped and prayed and believed would happen—a Tadyawan church! We had confidence that the Lord would add to His church, and we wondered who would be next to defy the demons and declare his faith in Jesus Christ. Sadly enough we knew it wouldn't be Bilbino. Though he was the leading figure in God's plan of preparation for the Tadyawan tribe, it was evident that for the present the church would be built without him.

14 Weather-beaten

Rain and more rain! Dode and I looked at it in disgust
from under the roof of our Tadyawan–Tawbuid house. It
was a new house, about fourteen by thirty feet and built
about five feet off the ground. It was a community effort
and could rightly be called a community house, for when
we visited their area, the Tadyawan and Tawbuid left their
permanent homes and, carrying their food, blankets, and
babies in huge rattan baskets strapped to their heads,
came to live with us. We were a happy crowd—Dode and
I, twenty-five Tadyawan, thirty Tawbuid, dogs, cats, a pet
monkey, and thousands of cockroaches, which when not
biting on some crumb, bit the people.

In clear weather the sun shone cheerfully through the
bamboo slats of the flooring and the window holes in the
bark wall, brightening the whole house and the spirits of
us all. But during a typhoon, when all the forest outside
trembled in the wind and dripped in the pouring rain,
and everything inside got damp and mouldy and dank,
the house shrank into an overcrowded, noisy, drab
shelter, for doorway and windows were blocked with
leaves to keep out the rain, and everybody stayed home
all the time.

When the rains started on this visit, we had already
been with the Tadyawan and Tawbuid three weeks and
were beginning to get weary just from the normal
routine. Each morning and evening we had Bible study,
first for the Tadyawan and then through them for the
Tawbuid. Then there were the daily reading classes as well
as what we jokingly called our academic studies, like the

meaning of the calendar or the value of money. In the hours that remained we chatted with the people or checked our Tadyawan vocabulary or analysed the language, to determine its alphabet, or translated songs or worked on doctrine booklets. We enjoyed it all, but it kept us busy and at times weary.

For relaxation Dode and I usually grabbed a set of clean clothes and retreated to the river for a swim and a bath and some light chitchat. But when it rained? Well, one day of rain is cozy, even two days can be with the right psychological approach, but more than that begins to be a trial.

As the steady rain moved into its third day, we started to fret in spirit. Everything was beginning to annoy us. Those who ventured outside returned shivering and dripping all over the floor, water mixed with blood streaming off their legs and ankles from leech bites. Dogs burst in with muddy feet, stopping just long enough to splatter everyone and everything within three feet of the inevitable shake, and then dropping into a corner to perfume the air with that doggy wet-wool smell. The floor—where we all cooked, ate, slept, worked, and just lived—became a slippery, sloppy mess. Women sat around picking lice out of each other's hair. Nappy-less youngsters, who didn't like the forest as a "toilet" in any weather, shunned it now. Wet wood in the fireplaces smoked into our eyes. Even the cockroaches bit more piercingly. We needed a bath, our hair needed washing, and our nerves were tightening. We longed for a little privacy, just a few minutes to sit and stare into space with our thoughts.

But privacy never came. Something was always demanding our patient attention. Mabilis got an egg-sized lump over his right eye from slipping on a rock outside. We applied pressure. Pablo was cranky with an earache. Dode extracted a cockroach. Children were irritable and cried easily. Esther fought with baby brother over mother's milk. Mother looked to us for counsel. Young Lutero couldn't figure out a word in his reading primer. The interruptions seemed endless. And then impatience spawned a thought—an unwanted thought it was, but persistent just the same: *Why don't they leave us alone for a while?*

It was for me a shattering discovery, but all my missionary zeal was gone. I wanted to escape from the very people I had come to serve for the Lord's sake! I lay on the floor just to shut my eyes and escape for a few minutes. But tribal youngsters never took kindly to afternoon siestas. As they frolicked on the floor, every bounce made the bamboo resound in my head like a miniature explosion, not at all improving my disposition.

The rains continued and the tension mounted until Dode and I, who usually got along very well together, were giving each other short and snappy answers—or if we managed not to snap, spoke in icy tones. Though neither of us mentioned it, we noticed it in each other and in ourselves, but were too weary and strained to want to do anything about it.

On the fourth day the rains stopped occasionally, but only for brief minutes. Our hopes of a bath rose each time, only to fall to despairing depths when the rain once more pelted down on the palm-leaf roof. It was tantalizing.

But on the fifth day the breaks between the rainfalls were longer. The typhoon was passing. In one of the longer intervals we decided to chance a bath. Without cheerful tones or spirits we packed our clean clothes into plastic bags, grabbed our wash-cloths and soap, told the household we would be back soon, and slipped through the mud down the hillside to the riverbank. Though we went together, we were miles apart, heavily silent or polite with an icy kind of politeness.

We hurried along the rocks to a place hidden from public view. But no sooner had we put our plastic bags of clean clothes on one of the rocks, thinking to plunge into the water—clothes and all—than, completely unannounced, down the rain came again, a deluge in huge, cold drops!

In no time we were drenched and covered with goose-pimples. Shivering, we hugged ourselves, but were still cold. In an effort to get warm we began "running on the spot", doing "knees raise", arms bent at the elbows and knees kicking high into the rain-filled air, while the water streamed over our faces and necks and down inside our clothes. It was exactly what we needed, for suddenly we realized how ridiculous we must have looked—two white women 'way out there in no-man's-land, doing "knees raise" in the pouring rain. We both burst out laughing, with good hearty laughs, the kind that had become unfamiliar to us the past five days. Still laughing, we soaped down ourselves and the clothes on us, quickly rinsed in the drenching rain, and raced back to the house, dripping into it and making the floor more of a slippery mess than it had been. We took turns holding up a blanket to corner off an improvised dressing room, still laughing at ourselves, while the Tadyawan and Tawbuid looked on wonderingly.

How good it was to have the whole world right again, with us no longer disgusted with ourselves, each other or the tribal folks!

The Lord has such practical ways of coming to the rescue of His children. We were ready again in spirit for our part in the building of the Tadyawan and Tawbuid church.

15 In Snare-infested Territory

Often we wondered who else the Lord would add to the Tadyawan church, and when. We didn't know for sure, but we began to surmise that it might be Bisi. Almost overnight Bisi had turned from a disturber of peace at the meetings to an active and enthusiastic participator. Instead of going to sleep, he listened carefully; instead of talking while others tried to memorize the Scripture verses, he began to memorize and did it well. He was hopelessly shy, however, and could never answer any question during the lesson that we threw out to him, but he could always shout out the answer when we addressed our question to someone else.

One day his little mother, Sala, now separated permanently from Bilbino, said to us, "Bisi should be baptized; he is a good son now." Though not knowing what prompted the remark, we made mental note of her testimony. Some days later it was confirmed by one of his married sisters, Dolilaw. "Bisi is so different now that he is believing, not like he used to be," she commented. Impatiently we waited for Bisi to take the initiative to tell us about his faith in Christ and his desire for baptism, but weeks went by, and he never broached the subject, though he still received and responded to a lot of the teaching. Should we ask him about it? Or should we wait? What about the demons? Did his believing mean a complete renunciation of them and their activity? We wondered and kept on wondering for some time. And then . . .

"Kasayaw's dead," they announced to us when we returned to their hills after a long stay in our cottage on the plains. Kasayaw was one of Sala's relatives, a small man covered with ringworm and cockroach bites, who had come, accompanied by his wife and daughter, to visit Sala and her big family. During his stay he had become seriously ill and grew thinner and thinner and correspondingly weaker and weaker. When it became obvious to the Tadyawan that he was going to die, Bilbino ordered Pedro and some of the other men to carry him to another area so that they'd be free from the stalking of his spirit once he was dead. They believed, as the great-grandfathers had taught, that a dead relative often came back to try to take the soul of someone else for company in that other world.

Pedro and Mabilis and a couple of the others carried Kasayaw down the trail, far away from the house for his last moments of life. As they carried him, his breathing got more laboured. Sure now that they would never make it to the next mountain, they chose a tree stump with the right qualifications—big enough to hold the body and high enough to keep the wild pigs from getting it—and there they placed him while he breathed his last. Then they tied his corpse securely with vines and fled back to tell the others that he had died.

Fleeing in great fear from the houses they lived in, the whole group hid from Kasayaw's spirit in a hut they had previously decided on when they saw he couldn't live. There they planned to stay secretly for five whole days as was the custom, to give his spirit a chance to pass them by.

Later Pedro continued the story for us, with Mabilis

sitting nearby to fill in some of the details. "We spent one day in that escape house," he said, "eating only what we had managed to gather before he died. We were all too afraid to go out to the fields. The second day, with nothing to do, we lay about on the floor, wishing we had some better food to eat and seriously hoping that Kasayaw's spirit wouldn't find our hiding place and cause one of us to become sick and die. But then," he continued, "on the third day Mabilis and I were talking things over and we thought, 'We belong now to Our Father, and we shouldn't be afraid of the demons and the spirits of the dead. Why are we staying here with all the others?'"

He was excited now as he went on: "We decided to go out to the fields to get some food; so we fastened our knives in their sheaths around our waists and headed for the doorway. Everybody else got mad at us. They were really frightened and said that we would reveal their hideout, endangering them as well as ourselves. Kasayaw's spirit was still close at hand. Someone had heard it muttering during the night. They shouted and screamed at us, but we told them that we belonged now to Our Father, and the demons couldn't hurt us. So we went," he said, and then, with eyes sparkling, added, "Bisi and young Lutero went with us too and nothing happened to any of us!"

So Bisi *had* turned his back on the demon world! Not long after that we invited Neville Cooper, a colleague, to come to baptize Bisi. Lutero, we felt, being young and easily led, needed a few more years to prove his individual belief in the Lord.

The Tadyawan church was now a church of three. Would they strengthen each other to a constant renouncing of the things that they had always known and followed? Would they embrace all the will of God?

Mabilis was of marriageable age; in fact, had been for some time. Several years prior to our visiting them, Bilbino, his grandfather, had asked for a neighbouring Tawbuid girl as a prospective bride for him. With the parents' consent she was brought into the Tadyawan area and lived with them so that they could observe her work habits to see if she would be a good working wife for Mabilis. When we first met her, she was an irresponsible child, only a fourteen-year-old giggle. But before Mabilis had declared his faith in Jesus Christ and was still following the heathen customs, he went through the ceremony of divination to see if she was the right one for him. On the night of the ceremony he dreamed of a boa constrictor. As that was an evil omen, he asserted in the morning that he would not take her for his wife.

But now that Mabilis was a Christian, what would his attitude be? Having a husband or a wife was very important to tribespeople. To them, that is what life is. No one ever stayed single. But Mabilis knew God's Word said he could have only a Christian wife. Yet, where, if anywhere, would they find a Christian bride for him? There were only three declared Christians among the Tadyawan—he, Pedro and Bisi. Now what? Would he weaken? Or would he hold to God's principle just as fervently as he had formerly held to the heathen principles? We were concerned.

"Could Mabilis marry a Christian girl even if her parents didn't believe?" Pedro asked one day while the others perked up to hear our answer. We assured him that the only thing relevant was the faith of the girl involved, not that of her parents.

"But it's hard to find girls for our young men," interjected Bilbino in mournful tones. "There are so few girls around in any case, let alone a Christian."

We agreed. "The reason there are so few girls around is that you strangle many of them while they're still babies. Isn't that so?" They laughed at our logic.

"But it's going to be hard to find a wife for Mabilis," they reaffirmed.

"Well, let's pray and ask Our Father to give him a wife. Our Father wants us to pray to Him about everything."

Mabilis was to have a long wait, but he waited, and during the waiting period he was tested. A very attractive girl came with her mother to visit in our area. She had run away from her first husband and was now looking for another one. What better choice than Mabilis? The Tadyawan liked her and thought the two would make a good match. She began coming to the meetings to hear the Word of God. They were encouraged to think that she would believe and then everything would be settled. Soon we began to hear her name associated with Mabilis's. It made us shudder. Everything was moving too fast. An agreement would have been too premature.

Our fears were turned into praise, however, for one day we were all sitting inside the house chatting about everything pertaining to their forest world, when we overheard someone saying to Mabilis, "Why don't you take her for your wife? She's a nice girl. And she's coming to the meetings. She'd make a good wife for you, Mabilis." We looked toward Mabilis and strained our ears above the racket of the rest of our large family.

Mabilis, sitting in the doorway, steadily gazed into the open for a while and, with convincing tones, said, "Don't rush me; I'm waiting for Our Father."

But the girl had no intentions of waiting. In her hurry for another husband whether by fair means or foul, she began flirting with Bilbino's oldest son, who was already married. Others beside ourselves became concerned, but the problem was resolved one bright day when a loud-mouthed Tadyawan from another area came into our mountains and demanded this girl as his own, adding her to the three wives that he already had. She seemed happy to go along with him.

Mabilis's chances for a bride now were nil. But he held to God's principle and busied himself with teaching the Tawbuid the Word of God.

In contrast, Pedro was fading into the background, with the light gone and the enthusiasm dulled. He still came to all the meetings, helped with language study, and had a friendly attitude, but a cloud was there, obscuring the openness that we had come to appreciate in Pedro. What was it? Had we offended him? Had someone else offended him? Did he have a weighty problem? Something was blocking his joy in the Lord. We didn't have to know what it was. We only prayed that the Lord would come to his rescue and release him from whatever it was that was choking off his vitality in the things of God.

One clear morning the house was full of brown bodies for Bible study. Every day we reviewed our memory verses together, then learned a new one. That morning our verse was I John 1.9—"If we confess our sins, he is faithful and just to forgive us our sins and to cleanse us from all unrighteousness." As usual, we pulled the verse apart for memorizing, explaining each phrase. I pointed out that Jesus' blood gives continual cleansing to the long-time Christian as well as to the new. At that, Pedro turned to us, incredulity written all over his face. "You mean that after we believe and are baptized, His blood will wash away any sin if we sin against Him?"

"Yes, exactly," we explained. "When we believe, His blood washes away all the past sin; but after we believe, we sometimes sin too because we are still in the body."

"Yes!" and Pedro was emphatic. "But you mean that His blood washes away that sin too?" Oh happy day for Pedro! Oh changed face! He jumped up with joy and shouted to the waiting Tawbuid, "Hey, you fellows, listen to what the two sisters have just taught us! They said that if we tell Our Father about our sin, Jesus' blood washes our inner beings every day and makes them clean. Listen to Mabilis teach you about that! Hurry, Mabilis, tell them!" Two excited voices explained the wonders of our merciful God. Two missionaries silently thanked God for that day of deliverance.

Not that that was the end of Pedro's problems. He had lots of them; folk jealous of his ability to grasp the Word of God so quickly, a wife trying to pull him back to heathen ways, and mean Filipinos taking advantage of him. We were all sitting around outside the house one day when a Filipino man came along, talked for a while and then took leave, dragging with him Pedro's lengths of rattan which with much sweat and great effort he had cut down in the forest. "I need this," was all the Filipino said as he took it.

"Hey," yelled Pedro's wife after him. "You can't take that—it's ours. That's stealing." He kept on walking, dragging after him the long pieces of rattan. What did he care for these ignorant people? He had a need. They had what he needed; so he took it.

"It's very difficult," said Pedro gloomily. "But it's always like that. They take anything of ours they want, and they never pay us for it, even though they've got more money than we'll ever have." Not even the news that Our Father kept a very accurate record comforted him.

The incident, moreover, reminded him of an even bigger problem. "It's hard," he reaffirmed in the same gloomy tone. "That Wakin we told you about is always after us too, taking what he wants or making us work for him. He promises to pay us, but he never does. He has evil thoughts toward our women too. He is cruel. Last week he beat me on my thigh. I had carried a note to him from one of his friends in town. When he read the note, because he didn't like what his friend had written, he beat me for delivering the note to him." He winced as he rubbed the palm of his hand over the sore muscle. "He is now threatening to kill me and Bogado," he proceeded. "Is it all right if we run away? Would Our Father be angry at that? We have prayed for Wakin, like you told us, but he doesn't change. He is wicked."

"It would be all right for you to run away provided you had some place to run to where you wouldn't starve. Where would you get food? All your fields are here," we reminded him.

"Well, then, would it be all right if we prayed that Our Father would make him go away?"

It was a timely question, because just prior to that time our workers with the Alangan tribe, Morven Brown and Daphne McKenzie, had had a similar experience of one man who made life exceedingly miserable for the Alangan tribesmen. They too had prayed that God would remove him from the area because he was not only mean but threatened the believers. In a very sobering way God answered the prayer by causing a landslide during heavy rains that sent that man's house crashing down the hillside, killing him and others that were in the house.

Bogado's eyes were wide when we finished telling that story. "Why don't we do that? Let's ask Our Father to send a typhoon that will demolish Wakin's house and kill him?" He giggled with sheer joy at the thought of having so menacing an enemy dealt with forever. He was disappointed when we contradicted him, telling him that we could pray to Our Father to remove Wakin from the area, but it was up to Our Father to choose His own method.

"But can we run away if he is still here?" persisted Pedro.

"Yes, it would be all right. But what about the Tawbuid? It seems as if Our Father has given you the responsibility of evangelizing the group. How will they hear if you move too far away? We're going home to our country soon, and you'll be the only ones around to help them, and they need to hear and understand His Word so that they'll believe and follow Him."

16 Sabil Obeys the Beautiful Spirit

While Dode was at home in Canada and I in the USA, the Lord proved Himself worthy of our confidence. Using the Tadyawan Christians, He added to His church a group of people, who like them had been prepared for the coming of the gospel through a prophecy.

Several mountain ridges away from the Banos River, Kalobang lay sprawled out in the large swing, his legs dangling over the sides, gently pushing against the bamboo floor to keep the swing in motion. His wife Sabil brushed around the inside of a blackened cooking pot to rid it of cockroaches, gave it a bang against the floor to insure its cleanliness, and filled it with freshly dug sweet potatoes. Everybody else in the house was gathered about

Kalobang's two sons, who were sitting on the floor facing each other, their right hands clasped together chin high, their mouths clamped firmly shut, wrist wrestling. With their left hands tightly clutching poles of the house for support, they skirmished to see who could get the right hand of the other down on to the floor first. Their movements shook the whole house more violently as time went on, for the household egged them on with cheers and shouts of advice. The older men concealed their amusement over these two boys fast becoming men; the other young boys sat with eyes flashing, waiting to challenge the winner. It was a pleasant racket silenced only occasionally by the tenseness of a deadlock. The suspense of those moments was relieved by the chanting of Kalobang in the background, his head turned slightly toward them all so that he could keep a proud eye on his two sons.

"Married couples, do not get angry with each other very often;
Children, listen to your parents;
Do not steal anything; always keep your promises;
Be kind to people; don't holler at them.
All help each other; do not fight with one another."

He stopped rocking and called to Sabil, "I wish everybody would follow that teaching. We'd all have a good life if they did." But before he finished speaking the din had started again.

"Shut up, everybody! I can't hear my husband's words," called out Sabil with her harsh, commanding voice. She had spoken. The wrestling stopped immediately, and the two boys scuttled back against the wall. The others settled down, young and old, married and single. They respected Sabil's right to reign, for her wise-one had given her power to whip the spirits of dead people, lessening their visits in that community.

"What did you say?" she asked of her husband, as she sliced the snake on the floor pole, and dropped the pieces into a pot of boiling water.

"I said," Kalobang repeated, "that if everybody followed that good teaching, we would all be happy and have a good life, and not have to be afraid of anybody."

"Sure," agreed Sabil, "but where would you find a whole group of people who would follow it? You know yourself how you and the others walked all over this island hunting for a place where all the people were kind and good, but you never really found any, remember? After looking all over the Aglobang area and then the Pola area, this is the best you could find—and even here on the Malyo River, not all the people are kind. We are the only ones who do the right thing all the time."

Kalobang grunted agreement and mentally reviewed all those days when he and the other men tramped the forest hoping to find a peaceful neighbourhood. He remembered the sweat, the fatigue, the hunger, the fears among hostile people, the disappointment at not finding what they were looking for, and then the final resignation to life as it always was, one continual slogging through the murky schemes of demons and men.

"But what about that spirit you told us of?" asked Panot, thick curly hair crowning wide eyes staring into the fireplace. "Didn't you tell us that Sabil saw a beautiful spirit who taught her good things and told her that some day strangers would come to teach that same kind of good teaching?"

"That's right," affirmed Kalobang. But he was quickly

drowned out by his wife's overlapping remarks. His meek and gentle temperament let her take control.

"Yes," she barked, "I was the one who saw that spirit. It *was* a beautiful one, and it taught me good things. Those words my husband was singing earlier were the words the good spirit taught me. It told us to teach our children those words too so that they would grow up to be good and to obey us. That's why we're always teaching the two boys and their younger sister. We want our three children to grow up right, doing good all the time."

"That spirit said we should teach them steadily," Kalobang added.

"Yes," Sabil clarified, "it said that we should teach them a little bit every day, not just every once in a while."

"I think it was a good spirit and a well-informed one," meekly asserted Kalobang.

Quickly Sabil cut him off again. "It surely was. It saw Kalobang's thoughts before he ever told anyone what he was thinking."

Kalobang winced. He knew what was coming next and giggled his embarrassment. Sabil continued, her loud, sharp voice piercing every sensitive ear in the room. "Kalobang saw a nice young girl in our village. We were already married at that time, but he had thoughts about that young girl. The good spirit told me about it; Kalobang hadn't said anything, but that spirit knew, and it told me what Kalobang was thinking. The spirit told me I should warn my husband not to think like that any more, that it was wrong. Here are the spirit's words, 'Even thinking it, the basket is already made.'" Her sharp eyes flashed around the room as her tones of finality seemed to curse the very air, pronouncing doom on anyone else who would similarly be guilty of the deed just through the thought of it, and especially on her husband,

who had better never think that way again about a young
girl.

Knowing pairs of eyes shot looks from one to another
around the room, their mouths silently sniggering over
Kalobang's naughtiness. What tribal man in those
mountains could plead innocence in such a matter? Many
had not stopped at the thought. But while not regarding
Kalobang as particularly evil, they dared not take sides
with him against Sabil.

After a few moments of embarrassed silence, Panot got
back to his original thought. "But didn't you say," he
drawled, "that that spirit had said something about other
teachers? Who will they be?"

Kalobang nodded, waiting for Sabil, who waited for
nobody. "Yes," she explained, "that's right. It said that
some day strangers would come to these mountains of
ours and teach us the same good things it had been
teaching me. It said we should listen to the teaching of the
strangers and that we should obey it all. I still see that
spirit occasionally. On one occasion it told me that once
those good teachers got here, I would never see it again."

As no one knew what to say, no one said anything.
Everybody just thought. Then Panot, his big eyes
wandering all around the room, broke the sober silence
by tweaking his wife's big toe and commanding her to
get him some water. All the little family groups, by now
huddled around their own fireplaces, started chatting
among themselves. Panot's child-bride handed him the
bamboo tube of water. He rinsed out his mouth, spat the
water out between the leaf wall and the bamboo floor,
and then confided to his wife, "I wonder if her words are
lies."

"Whose words?" his young wife asked quietly.

"Kalobang's wife's. It's been such a long time. She saw

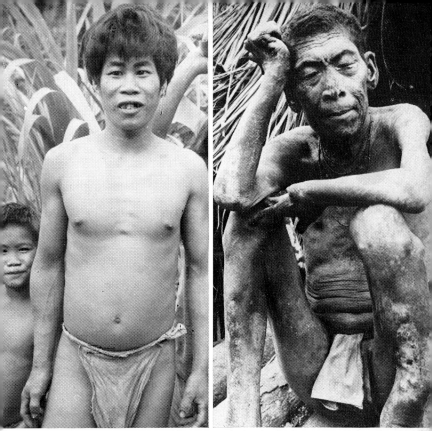

(*Left*) "Pedro boasted no natural beauty." (*Right*) Lindogayan: "Dressing his putrefying sores was a challenge to the strongest of stomachs." (*Below*) Bilbino, Sala and family: Bisi is on Bilbino's left, with Dolilaw in front of him.

Caroline enjoyed teaching "Our Father's Words".

"Fires crackled under blackened pots of rice or sweet potato."
Dode is cook for the day.

that spirit long before we ever met them. Why would it take so long for those strangers to get here?"

"Maybe they're coming from very far away," she suggested.

Panot smiled benevolently and raised his eyebrows, half admiring his little wife's cleverness. He liked her. She would make a good wife, he thought, better than all the others he had seduced and then dropped. He hoped they would have a large family.

Some weeks later Mapol returned home to Sabil's household when she and Kalobang were over on the next mountain visiting. "Hey, did anybody see that new house beside the river?" he asked with a voice that was much too little for his big brawny body.

"Where?" asked Panot.

"It's right beside the river just off the rocky beach. A Filipino has built it. I saw him when I was helping to build a dam the other day down by the river. He called it," and he paused, "I forget what he called it, but he didn't call it a house. They teach in it, or something like that, he said. One of the fellows from across the river said that he heard people singing in there. He didn't go too close, though."

"Oh, now I know," said Panot, light appearing in his bewildered eyes. "That must be what Sabil was talking about some time ago. She said that the Filipino teaches good words, tells people how to be kind to each other and everything. She thinks maybe this is what the spirit meant. She thinks we should all go and listen."

Fear dominated Mapol's eyes, and his chest expanded with a big breath. "Not me," he asserted. "You can go if you want to. Anyway, I wouldn't understand it because it's not in our language, is it? Do they know our tribal languages?"

"No, and none of us understand the Filipino's language. Some of us had better go, though, since Sabil said so."

Back on the Banos River, in our absence, the Tadyawan and Tawbuid visited each other frequently, enjoying each other's company and sharing in the things of God. Mabilis and Bisi, realizing the insatiable hunger of the Tawbuid for the Word, decided, with the approval of all, to leave the Tadyawan village and settle in the Tawbuid village so that they could teach them regularly. It was a happy arrangement for all, and the Tawbuid grew in their understanding of spiritual things.

In the midst of all their joys, however, there was an ominous cloud. A steadily growing stream of Filipinos invaded the mountains in quest of land, imposing on the tribesmen and taking advantage of them. It was a grievous burden, and the tribesmen's minds were troubled. For the Tadyawan there seemed only one solution. Living so close to the large river, they were too accessible to the outside world; they knew they would have to move deeper into the mountains, but, concerned for the neighbouring Tawbuid, they delayed their move. However, when Russell and Barbara Reed, feeling called by God, came to live and work among the Tawbuid, the Tadyawan felt free to make their move, this time farther back in the mountains and southward toward the Bansod River.

Settled along the Bansod, Bisi and Mabilis now helped Pedro with the teaching. They haltingly read from the booklets we had mimeographed. The papers were dirty now from much handling, and they had to squint to see the words; yet they kept on teaching morning and evening when all the families came home from their field work. And the people kept listening, crowded together on the floor, leaning against each other and trying to remember what was being taught.

"This page is on the Holy Spirit," Mabilis announced one morning. "That's what we'll be studying today. But first, let's sing a song."

"Yes, let's sing, 'Jesus is the Way'," spoke up Bisi, and there followed twenty-seven original, unharmonious cacophonous chants, some of the bodies swaying to the timing, others staring hard at their feet trying to remember the words. Mabilis, singing in his falsetto voice to imitate Dode and me, always lagged behind the others, jumbling everything together at the end to catch up.

"What does that mean?" he asked. "Is Our Jesus a path like one of our mountain trails? Dolilaw, you answer that." Dolilaw hated being called on in public, and this was no exception. She quickly flapped her ragged cape over her face and pushed hard against the wall with her back, wishing to be swallowed up by its leaves. Everybody waited. The cape was slowly removed, and she quickly giggled a "no" and then buried her face right into her husband's neck. Mabilis went on, the authority of the teacher being natural to him. "How is Our Jesus the way, then?" He directed his question to Lutero. Lutero's eyes shifted, and he tittered something to the person on his right. "Say it, Lutero; you know the answer," his older brother encouraged him.

"If we believe in Him, He takes us to heaven," mumbled Lutero.

"Good," said Mabilis. Then he picked up his booklet again, frowned at the words for some minutes, looked all around with bird-like movements, scratched his neck, rumpled his hair and then coughed a little cough, cleared his throat loudly and began, "Our Father's teaching on the Holy Spirit: The Holy Spirit is God too. He is the One who lives in our inner beings. He helps us to teach Our Father's words to others. Our Jesus told us to go and teach His words to other people so that they will go to His house and not to the big fire." He stretched the lesson to great lengths, questioning and correcting and instructing.

After the lesson, big, bulky Manindok pulled Mabilis aside. The big man towered over the slender young man as they talked. Manindok's long, unkempt hair made him look so wild. But in that solid barrel-chest lay a tender and responsive heart. He was too mentally dull to understand everything, but what he understood he wanted to obey. "Mabilis," he said, "I think I'd better go over to the Malyo River to teach my relatives over there. They have never heard Our Father's words. My niece is there and also my nephew Mapol and his family. The leader of the group is a woman who has a powerful wise-one; Sabil, I think her name is."

Sabil was snapping orders at the household as usual when the leaves in the doorway rustled and Manindok's big frame appeared. He squatted on the floor right by the entrance. The family had just finished eating, but managed to scrounge up a coconut shell full of cold leftover rice for the newcomer. Manindok ate with vigour after his long trek over the mountains.

"Is your harvesting all done?" they asked him as if it hadn't been many months since they had seen him.

"Yes, we're finished. What about you? Is your crop in?"

"Yes, but rats ate much of it. Never mind, the women have a good sweet potato crop this year. We won't be hungry. But next year we'd better make bigger fields."

"As big as Tandik's?" Manindok inquired, and then

noting that Tandik wasn't there, he asked, "Where is Tandik?"

"He's gone. The spirits ate his soul. He was spitting blood and got weaker and weaker. We were afraid of his spirit when he died," some of them replied, re-living the fear of those days.

"We're not afraid of spirits and demons any more," Manindok interjected shyly, but glad that he could get on to the subject that he wanted to talk about.

"What did you say?" several shouted at him.

"In our area we are following the words of Our Father in heaven. They are good words, and I have come to teach them to you. He says that if we follow His words, we will be walking on the narrow road that leads to His house, but if we don't follow what he says, we'll be walking on the big road that leads to a big fire. That's where the Devil lives. He is the chief of all the evil spirits and demons. That's their home."

Fearful news this, and they were all confused. The Devil? Narrow road? Big road? A big fire? What was he talking about?

"Who taught you all that?" they asked of him.

"Our sisters," he answered. "But they're not here now. They've gone back to their land. They gave us papers which we study, and that's what the papers say. The teaching is from Our Father up there in heaven."

"Who's the elder in your village, and does he believe this too?"

"His name is Bilbino, and he says he believes, but he doesn't really yet because he still listens to his wise-one, and he is afraid of the demons and spirit. We are not afraid of them, for Our Father protects us from them."

"Don't you get sick then any more?" they asked, much

interested. Some had even scuttled over quite close to him.

"Yes," said Manindok, "we still get sick, but we don't sacrifice to the demons any more, and we don't chant. We just pray to Our Father to make us well."

"Do your people steal?"

"Not the ones who are believing in Our Father, for he says it is wrong to steal and that He will punish those who do. They'll go to the big fire."

"We don't steal either," broke in Sabil. "Some people around here do, but we don't. We don't fight either." None of the others commented, knowing that was only a half-truth. There was never room for argument; Sabil was always right, and they couldn't win over her, although some of the more rebellious made futile attempts.

"That's the kind of teaching," continued Sabil, "that I heard once from a beautiful spirit. And it's the same kind of teaching that we hear now when we go down to that house by the river. It's hard to understand what they say because it is not our language, but they sing and are kind to us."

"Heaven is a nice place," insisted Manindok, "but we have to believe in Our Father if we want to go there."

"Will I have my wife in heaven?" Panot inquired.

Manindok didn't know the answer to that, but he told them the things that he did understand. His limitations, however, were no match for their interest.

Back home again on the Bansod he explained it all to Mabilis. "They are interested and want to hear more. They told me to come back again, but I can't teach very well because I don't understand it all myself. I've taught them all that I could. But they asked me so many questions I couldn't answer that I think it would be good if you went along with me next time. You could carry your papers and teach them everything they want to know. I forget very much of what you teach me. I wish I knew how to read."

"I'll help you," replied Mabilis eagerly, "and I'll go along with you to teach them. When shall we go?"

"I told them we'd be back after the moon finished bathing in the sea," he explained.

"All right," said Mabilis, "we'll go then."

Manindok and Mabilis made several visits to that area. All the while Kalobang and Sabil and the others were doing some thinking. These men had talked of two sisters who came from another place to their island. Were these the people the good spirit meant many years ago? Sabil had thought it was that Filipino man who had built that house, but he wasn't much of a stranger. Maybe these women were the ones. One day the matter was finally settled; she had another visitation from the spirit, and she asked it if they should listen to the teaching of the women, or if they should stay where they were and go to hear the teaching of the Filipino man. The spirit's answer was that they should go to live in Manindok's area and follow the teaching of the women. For Sabil there was no other answer. The spirit had said they should go; therefore, they would go.

The next time Mabilis and Manindok visited them, Kalobang said, "We'd like to come and live with you people so that we can hear your teaching every day."

"You can all come if you like, and we'll be happy to teach you all we know ourselves. The sisters will be coming back in a few moons, and they'll be able to teach you even better than we can. They don't know all our language yet, but they pray and ask Our Father to help them. Sometimes they make mistakes, but we understand what they're trying to say. You'll learn lots when they teach you."

It was all the invitation they needed. A short time later Sabil's large household packed their belongings into their rattan baskets and started the hike over the mountains and through the rivers to their new home on the Bansod. They were five families in all, and Mabilis noticed that Manindok's attractive and vivacious niece was in the crowd of movers.

17 "I Want You if You Want Me"

On the North American continent, Dode and I had no idea of the exciting things happening in our Tadyawan mountains. As the days sped by and we peeled month after month off our calendars, we wondered what we would find when we returned. And then we peeled the month of April, 1964. Furlough was over. We were due to return.

Dode and I met in San Francisco, there boarding our ship for the Philippines. We arrived in Manila in the heat of mid-June, the mugginess enveloping us and the city's wind-whipped dust soon clinging to our perspiring skin and clothes. Riding along in the OMF's Volkswagen van, we passed squatters' shacks and grand hotels and sidewalks busy with people. Hand-painted "jeepneys" with their loads of trim and starched passengers zig-zagged through traffic, whizzing past us, cutting in front, pushing us out of line, or beeping us on to greater speed. Manila was her usual self.

Because our hearts were a hundred miles to the south, where our imaginations could already see activity in a jungle clearing, we remained in the big bustling city only long enough to clear our baggage through customs and to have our entry papers validated. Leaving the city on a big wooden bus, we lumbered southward. After a half-day's ride we neared the Batangas pier and could see the inter-island boat dipping lightly in the calm sea, waiting for its noon-hour sailing time to Mindoro. Many of its passengers were already aboard.

It was a clear day, its brightness livening the colour of sky, sea and the small mountainous islands we passed on the three-hour trip to Calapan. The calm sea promoted a leisurely atmosphere aboard, though the ship was bulging with people and cargo. Most of the way Dode and I sat thinking to ourselves about the Tadyawan and what lay ahead. We had pretty well talked ourselves out on the subject on the Pacific, but now, with Mindoro so close, we silently went over everything again, speculating on the news the Tadyawan would have for us and planning for the next four years.

"Dode, ol' girl," I said, breaking into a long silence, "you know, somehow we're going to have to add elementary Tagalog classes to our schedule."

"That's right, or the Tadyawan will never be able to attend the tribal Bible school." Bible school! We both had to smile at the almost incredible thought of Tadyawan in Bible school. Only four years before, these G-stringed forest people had known nothing of the Lord, only the fear of demons.

The development of a tribal Bible school had been set in motion at the mission's field conference just before our furlough. Since all six tribes on the island spoke separate languages, Tagalog, now known as "Filipino", the national language of the Philippines, was chosen as the teaching medium. Now we were wondering, with a church of only three baptized believers, who would learn Tagalog well enough eventually to attend with profit.

"But we don't want their ability to learn Tagalog to be the deciding factor, do we?" Dode stated, more than asked.

I agreed. "No, it's got to be those who show gifts of evangelism and teaching, like Mabilis."

Then we thought of the complications. What if prospective students were married, with little children? And if they were to leave their fields, what would they do for food? Questions came faster than answers. But, we concluded, these would be questions the church would have to answer—when we had a functioning church.

We were now getting close enough to Calapan to see trucks and buses waiting on the pier. People around us began securing their bags and boxes, tidying their hair, and awakening children stretched out on camp cots. As the boat pulled alongside the wharf, while it was still in motion, rough *cargadors* in faded denims and open shirts began leaping on board, their bare feet gripping the ship's rail and then thudding to the deck. Vying with each other for customers, they darted from one passenger to another shouting, "Can I carry your baggage?" Heckling and bargaining followed. By the time the boat was anchored and the gangplank was lowered, heavily laden *cargadors* and passengers surged together toward the exit gate, and the disembarking degenerated into a hectic scramble of pushing, shoving, jabbing and cursing. We sighed with relief at the bottom of the gangplank and gladly guided our *cargadors* to a small horse-drawn *kalesa*. Once we were in and headed for our mission's head-quarters for tribal work, we let the rhythmic *thlot, thlot* of the horse's hooves on the blacktop steady our slightly jangled nerves.

The next morning after a too-short visit to our superintendent, his wife, and others at the hillside headquarters, we caught a bus and rattled and bumped our way southward to the town of Pinamalayan, where we would make our base.

In Pinamalayan, as we busied ourselves unpacking and settling in, we kept wondering, silently or out loud, when we would see the Tadyawan. They had, we heard, moved to the Bansod River, making it impossible for us to find them on our own. They would have to come for us. But we knew they would come, for they had visited other missionaries in town several times recently inquiring about our arrival date.

Four days later, when dusk was putting a damper on all the town's activities except the amplified juke boxes, we heard voices on our tiny porch. Tadyawan! We hurried to the open door and there stood Mabilis, Pedro, and a couple of others. Our words spilled out in rapid succession, our voices high-pitched with excitement. The Tadyawan, confused by our fanfare, remained composed and answered questions flung at them with their usual short, cryptic answers. Yes, they had continued the daily Bible studies. The three baptized ones taught the lessons. Yes, they had taught the Tawbuid daily until the Reeds had arrived to help. No, they hadn't been pushed off their land. Yes, Wakin was still around making trouble. Yes, two more were ready for baptism—Lutero and Manindok, who had renounced all practices connected with the demons and were wholly following Our Father.

"And what about evangelistic trips?" we asked. "Did anybody take the teaching to others?"

"Oh, yes, and there are some who want to believe; in

fact, some have moved into our area so that they can hear the teaching all the time." And they beamed the smile of satisfaction at a job well done.

We glanced in the direction of the stranger with them. "Is this one of the new ones?" we asked, hoping not to frighten him by calling attention to him.

"Yes," they said matter-of-factly. "And there are more too, some of them are relatives of Manindok. They're much interested in Our Father's words. Some are already following and have nothing more to do with demons." They couldn't miss the pleasure written all over our faces. "It's too soon to baptize them, though," one of them cautioned. "They need to have more teaching from you. We've taught some of them to read, and they've caught on very quickly. They are five couples in all, some with children."

"Where do they live?" we wanted to know.

"Well, they've built their houses about two hours away from us—but they have built one big house near ours to stay in when they come on Sundays to listen to our teaching." The spokesman paused and then, "When will you be ready to come in and meet them?" he asked.

We set the date and in a few days were eagerly accompanying them into the familiar hills. June had been a rainless month. The leaves on the trees were yellow, the crops anaemic, the roads powdery, and the mountain trails hard and dry. Not a leech was to be seen. We drank quarts of water as we plodded over the trails, heavy and weary from being out of practice. The hiking hours dragged on. But just when exhaustion had slowed our climb to a near stop, the crow of a rooster encouraged us—we knew we were getting close. A rooftop pointing through the foliage above us confirmed the fact. A few more somewhat lightened steps, and we were home!

Home—theirs and ours—was the usual low grass-roofed bamboo, bark and pole structure, this one built long and narrow. Just fifty deep breaths away stood another house, bigger and higher. That was the weekend home of the five new families who came bag and baggage every weekend for Sunday meetings.

So eager were we to meet the new families that it seemed as if Sunday would never come. But it did, and with it the new additions to the congregation. In response to the children's usual clobbering of the piece of cast iron that served as a bell, they made their way up the narrow trail from their weekend house to ours. Sabil, being one of the first to arrive, took it upon herself to arrange the seating, barking orders at each member of her group as they made their entrance through the doorways. Immediately we dubbed her "The Duchess", only learning her real name later.

It was a full house, with brown body against brown body sitting upright mid-floor, draped over neighbours, slumping against walls or poles, and filling doorways and windows. Naked children hung on to the necks of parents or grandparents or squirmed in laps or walked about from one adult to another demanding attention—and getting it. It was stifling, but we got the church service under way. The sermon, however, never reached its prepared conclusion, for the new folk had many questions to ask. We sat for hours in discussion. Heads bobbed, mouths yawned, eyes drooped and closed. But the keen ones persisted in asking their questions until they understood what they wanted to know.

Manindok's niece, Atla, was in the crowd that day. We liked her as soon as we saw her. She was alive with vitality, the life of the party. Her resounding voice came through clear and strong and happy. Sparkling eyes lit her plain, broad face. She was everybody's friend, and in no time ours too.

Atla worried us, though, as time went on, for her interest seemed not so much in the Word of God as in our two young men, Bisi and Mabilis, both eligible for marriage and both prospects for Bible school. How could they resist that free and radiant personality of hers? Those lovely, dark eyes followed them, and they were the objects of her prettiest, coyest smiles and her wittiest remarks. We wondered which one she would eventually concentrate on.

Before very long we realized it couldn't be Bisi, for we began to hear his name coupled with Kasosok's. Tadyawan gossip told us they were interested in each other, although no formal arrangement had been made. Then one day one of the children pushed into our hands a crumpled piece of paper covered with dirty fingerprints. "Bisi wants you to read this," they chorused.

The note read: "To Kasosok. The one writing is Bisi. I want you if you want me." Turning the paper over we read his simple postscript: "But I don't want you if you haven't left your old life."

Kasosok didn't disappoint him. Though not yet baptized, she was a believer and wanted him if he wanted her. His was the first written proposal of marriage in the history of the Tadyawan tribe. And it was followed by the first Christian wedding.

After the wedding ceremony, the Tadyawan sat around asking us questions, mostly about how we courted and married in America. The questions led nicely to a subject that had caused us concern for some time. It was the matter of sleeping arrangements. The Tadyawan slept side by side on the floor, huddled together to keep warm, husbands and wives, brothers and sisters, young boys and girls. We had noted that Atla slept at our house and always saved a place for Mabilis beside her.

"Another thing that is different in America," I inserted, "is that young men and their girl friends who want to please Our Father never sleep side by side, even with other people around. It's too big a temptation to sin against Our Father."

"I agree," spoke up Bisi; and then because his remark gave him away, he dropped his chin on to his chest in embarrassment. As my eyes roamed around the room, I saw Mabilis thoughtful, his eyes staring vaguely at nothing.

Later, when our evening service was over and the new families had gone to their house, the young people played outside in the bright moonlight. One by one, as they tired, they came in, dug for their blankets tucked in the palm roof, and settled down for the night. About ten o'clock Atla bounced into the house, laughing and giggling with another of the young girls. Dode and I were already in our sleeping bags, but we weren't asleep; and though the fire was dying down, it was still bright enough for us to see. They chose sleeping space near one of the fireplaces, Atla leaving a space for Mabilis as usual.

Later, when all was quiet and almost everybody either asleep or nearly asleep, we felt the house shake and knew someone was coming up the pole. It was Mabilis. He crouched through the doorway which was close to the fireplace where Atla was waiting. He stopped, turned his back to the fireplace, and like a silhouetted statue remained hunched in the doorway, staring out into the night. Dode and I poked each other through our sleeping bags. There, surely, was a young man fighting a spiritual battle, whether to obey the teaching he had heard that afternoon or to follow the ways that were so very normal for a Tadyawan. "Lord, help him make the right decision," we prayed desperately and kept on praying for the whole eternal three minutes he stayed there motionless.

When Mabilis moved, he moved quickly. Dislodging his blanket from the palm shingle just above the door, he stepped lightly but with determination right across the house to the other side, dropped to the floor, and pulled his blanket over him for the night. His battle was won. He loved Atla, it was evident. But he intended to obey the Lord.

In the days that followed Mabilis basked in the warmth of Atla's charm and attention and, like a cock, he showed off in response at every opportunity.

18 Bilbino Held Fast

But while Mabilis spent happy days full of hope for the future, one isolated hut held sorrow. Bilbino and his young second wife faced the inevitable as they saw their tiny baby girl unresponsive. They had lost their first baby while we were home on furlough, and now they reckoned they would lose this one too. She refused to drink her mother's milk, and her whole body turned an odd colour. Though they had cut themselves off considerably from the others and from us, choosing to stick with the demon culture of their fathers, they now thought of us and decided to bring the baby to us for medicine.

Dode, her usual tender self, doctored the baby as well as her nurse's training allowed. But as Bilbino, girl wife,

Manindok and his wife: "I was cursed. . . . Nine of our children have died"—but three more are living.

Kalobang, Sabil and family: "If everybody followed that good teaching we would all be happy."

"They were proud of their new church and the small 'parsonage' (*left end*), and we were too."

"We knew we'd have a full house at church that day."

and baby disappeared through the door, Dode shook her head. She wasn't at all sure the little one would recover.

Dode was right in her doubt. Four days later the beaten mother, unwashed, hair uncombed, and despair on her face, carried her dirty little bundle to our house again. We peeped at the little form in the rag. The baby was still alive, but barely, bleeding from nose and ears, its ashen body limp and motionless. When Bilbino arrived a few minutes after his wife, we felt we should prepare them for the baby's death.

Not wanting the demons to see his disappointment, Bilbino giggled characteristically, his lips hidden behind short, stubby fingers. His wife was less successful at pretending. A few unwanted tears fell down her dirty cheeks, ever so quietly; but brushing the tears quickly away, she clutched her little bundle more tightly, intermittently stealing glances inside. No one else in the house offered any comfort. They laughed and joked and carried on life as usual, finally urging us to start the reading and writing lessons.

We began to teach with divided hearts, keeping an eye on the heart-broken mother. All of a sudden we noticed that she had joined the crowd and was bending over someone's shoulder, gaily poking fun at the mistakes he was making. Wondering what she had done with the baby, we glanced around and spotted a little lump hanging in the cloth hammock. Oh, the coldness demons demanded at death! We looked from the little lump to the mother, who was forcing herself to watch the pages which she couldn't read. "Is your baby gone?" we asked her quietly. She jerked her head meaning "no" and hastily returned her eyes to the pages again, raising one hand to hide her face. She knew the end was near.

About an hour later Pedro's unbelieving wife dared to

approach the hammock. "It's gone!" she screeched and joined the laughter coming from various corners of the house. Scooting back to her place, she said to her two-year-old son, "Go, grab what's in the swing. You'll have fun playing with that toy. It's like a little old lady." The toddler hesitated, but some of the other children ran over and with outstretched fingers gave the tiny corpse a poke. Now adults took turns looking into the hammock, each making some heartless remark. "Look how loose its skin is!" Or, "Hey, everybody, look at its chin, it's practically gone." And Bilbino and his wife joined in the merriment, not wanting the demons to see their grief.

That night, when the warmth of the fire dispelled some of the coldness of the afternoon's experience, we suggested to Bilbino and his wife that we have a church funeral for the baby. Reluctant at first, they acquiesced when we told them they didn't have to take part in any way.

The next day was dark and rainy, the kind of a day that makes funerals anywhere more gloomy. But there was no apparent gloom here. Bilbino sat for a long time tying together some pieces of bark to form a little coffin. His wife and another woman had gone off to dig a grave. When the tiny body was placed into the crude container and Bilbino had secured it with vines, he suggested that we all go to the grave. We had a short service first, Bilbino drinking in every word we voiced about death and the beauty of it when we belong to Our Father. We felt sure God spoke to his stubborn heart that day.

After the service the whole community marched single file down the mountain path to the field where the two women were digging and having a hilarious time doing it—or at least pretending they were having a hilarious time. "Be sure to dig it deep enough so that she doesn't smell," someone in the funeral procession called. The comment poured cold water on us, but everybody else laughed. By this time the women had hit the roots of a cassava plant. "What a pity!" someone mourned, others joining him, "look what you've done to the cassava! Now it won't be any good for eating." They managed, however, to control their laughter long enough to sing one of our choruses and to pray quietly as we placed the little coffin into its grave.

After that, while most of the people went on with their day's work we went back to the house, silently depressed; our only encouragement was the thought that God seemed to be trying to speak to Bilbino about his unyieldingness, through all this. Later in the day, in fact, Bilbino came over to our fireplace with questions about heaven and the new life. The direction of the conversation paved the way to express what was in our minds. "Bilbino," I asked, "do you think God is wanting to say something to you? Do you think maybe He is punishing you for your disobedience to Him?" The broad-shouldered but ageing man thought a moment, then admitted that he himself had wondered. He was softening, it seemed.

"Won't I go to heaven now that I've taken another wife?" he inquired, concern written all over his face.

"Taking her was disobedience to Our Father, all right," I conceded. "But what is going to keep you from heaven is the fact that you don't really believe Him."

"But I do believe Him," he insisted.

"What about your connections with the demons and your wise-one?" we countered.

"Oh, I believe them too." He was defensive now. "I have to follow what they say, for they would punish me if

I didn't. Their teaching is good, just like yours from Our Father. But I follow what Our Father says, too."

"But it can't be!" we pleaded. "You cannot have Our Father and the demons. He says that we should not have anything to do with them, that He should be the one we listen to."

"But my wise-one tells me what's going to happen in the future, and he gives me power to heal sicknesses or to stop the rain if I want to. He would be angry if I didn't listen to him any more."

"Then you don't really believe Our Father." It was all we could say. Bilbino's will had yet to be conquered, and the Holy Spirit would have to be the one to do it.

19 Under Attack

Mabilis looked dejected, scratching his head and frowning. It was obvious that he had something on his mind, for he had stopped reading sometime earlier and just sat glumly staring at the bamboo floor, or casting occasional glances at us. We were helping Pedro and Manindok with their reading problems. Off to one side Bisi was helping his wife Kasosok to improve her writing. Others were bent over their books by the light of the windows. Outside, Bilbino's voice rose above the crowd as he dramatically recounted an interview he had had with a leader of another group.

"He was really mad at me," explained Bilbino, laughing now that he was away from the old man. "He said that my oldest daughter had laughed at their dog when she passed their house. Now he wants me to pay him something to cure the curse she put on them by laughing."

Those listening to Bilbino stormily raised their objections, but he put them to silence. "Sure, I know the old man's wrong. It's true that the great-grandfathers taught us that it's wrong to make fun of animals, but they told us that those who make fun bring a curse on themselves, not on the owners of the animal."

This time his listeners' voices rose reassuringly. Bilbino was encouraged to go on with his tale. "I argued with him," he bragged. "Yes, I did; I didn't care if he was older than me. He was wrong and I let him know it. I just told him, 'You have forgotten the teachings of the great-grandfathers. You are not cursed by her laughing. We are the ones cursed. I am not going to pay you anything.'" He paused and then added, "You know, I think he was just using this episode to get a new knife or something."

"But did Older Sister really make fun of his dog?" anxiously asked Dolilaw, one of the younger sisters.

"Yes, but don't worry about it," comforted Bilbino. "We won't be cursed. I've taken care of it with my wise-one. He's already dealt with the demons over the curse. Nothing will happen to us."

We raised our eyebrows. Mabilis addressed us, though he continued staring at the floor. "We've got to pray for Bilbino. If he doesn't believe, we'll never be able to convince anybody else that they should believe. Whenever we go on evangelistic trips, the people always ask us, 'Does your leader believe?' and as soon as we say 'no', they don't want to listen to any more of our teaching."

"But why?" we asked.

"Because every Tadyawan listens to his leader. If not, he is considered a bold rebel, and nobody wants to have anything more to do with him. We Tadyawan never act independently; we always do what our leader says. When we tell them that Bilbino doesn't believe yet, they call us brazen offspring and lecture us on following our customs."

"Has he shown any signs of being close to believing?" we hopefully asked.

Mabilis, still frowning heavily, picked up his book and slid it into his plastic bag. "Sometimes he does, but sometimes when you're not around, he makes fun of us for believing. He says he won't stop us if we want to believe, though. He claims that his wise-one is as mighty as Our Father. The other day when it was raining, he stopped by the house and taunted us, saying, 'Go ahead, pray to Our Father; ask Him to stop the rain. *I* can make it stop if I want to because my wise-one taught me the words. But you go ahead. Let's see you do it.'"

"Did you pray?" we asked.

He stood up, grabbed his plastic bag of books, and tucked it into the wall, high out of the reach of the small children; but, as if on second thought he remembered that the young scamps around the place were born pole-climbers, he gave the bag a further poke so that none of the plastic would show. He turned toward us, "No, we didn't pray, because it didn't matter to us whether it rained or not. There was no reason to pray for it to stop. It's different during a typhoon though. When pelting rain and strong wind pound against these bark walls, we pray a lot."

"We sure do," piped up Lutero. "All the sugar cane in my field was blown over during the last typhoon; Mabilis lost lots of his rice; and Mapol's sweet potato field was buried under an avalanche of mud from the mountainside. One of the other new fellows thought he'd lose his rice, but the mountainside only cracked open and never really came down. We did a lot of praying at that time. And, incidentally, some of the new people are ready for baptism. They mentioned it to me the other day. They really are walking now with Our Jesus and want to be baptized. They were afraid of baptism before, but now that they have seen me and Manindok baptized, they aren't afraid."

It was a wonder they weren't afraid, I thought, after seeing Lutero and Manindok baptized, for their baptism was a bit rough. In a way, it was our fault, for, as our first attempt to get the church functioning as a church, we suggested that the three baptized men perform the actual baptism. Our only advice was to caution them about the weight of Manindok's bulky body. It was really no match for theirs. "Be careful," we warned, "when baptizing him. Plant your feet firmly in the stream's pool, and hold him tightly so that you don't let him slip over into the water."

On the morning of the baptism, Bisi looked apprehensive all during the service and then even more so down at the pool when he walked into the water to help Pedro baptize Manindok. At the appropriate moment, when Manindok had finished testifying to his faith, and when Pedro had placed his hands squarely on Manindok's body, Bisi quickly reached up, grabbed the front of Manindok's long hair, plunged him goggle-eyed into the water, and yanked him out again, all in a few seconds. Dode and I had all we could do to keep from bursting into gales of laughter. We should have known that Bisi would come up with something original and practical. He always did!

"Let's all pray about the baptisms," I suggested, coming back from the reverie that made me want to laugh all over again. "You five baptized ones will help us with the examining of the candidates. Let's ask Our Father to give us wisdom."

The sun was getting higher and beckoned them to the day's work. Lutero and Bisi grabbed their fishing goggles and spears, and, wrenching a banana each from the stalk hanging from the roof near the fireplace, made their way to the door. Kasosok jerked herself up and with high-pitched apology handed us her writing paper. She held her two hands over her mouth while we read, her eyes searching our faces for signs of approval. With a laugh, when we said it was good writing, she wheeled around, grabbed her basket and dashed out of the house.

We had been honest; it was good writing, but her theology left something to be desired. Writing a short composition on the verse, "Him that cometh to me I will in no wise cast out," she wrote, "That means that no matter who it is, he can come to Jesus. If he comes to Jesus, Jesus will not send him away. Whether it is a man, or a woman, or a child, if he comes to Jesus, Jesus will not tell him to go away. Even if the devil came to Jesus, Jesus would accept him."

Her heart was right anyway. We knew she was ready for baptism and hoped she would soon ask for it.

Outside, she called to some of the other women gaily, "Who's going to the field today?" While the women thought over their plans, she called again, "Come on, Atla, let's work in my field."

At the name of Atla, Mabilis's eyes shot to the opening in the wall, lighted up momentarily, and then became painfully mournful again. He looked in our direction.

"I'd like to have a *cinko's* worth of aspirin," he requested of us.

"Mabilis, you've been buying an awful lot of aspirin

lately. Do you share them with others, or are you taking them all the time?" we inquired, concerned.

"I get such severe headaches," he said. "My head sometimes pounds, so badly that at times I am deaf. That's why I take the aspirin. I eat them all the time, but still I've got the headaches."

As the days went on, we guessed that the headaches and deafness persisted. The expression on Mabilis's face grew strange, as if he were confused. When he taught Bible stories, there began to be a vagueness about them, and they lacked all his usual colour and careful detail. We asked him about it.

"It gets so bad," he explained, "that I temporarily forget who I am." Our concern mounted.

It mounted further the day they hurried Mabilis into town. We had been in Pinamalayan preparing our teaching materials and riding back and forth to Calapan to visit the government offices. We were trying to get all the information and application papers the Tadyawan needed for applying for a licence to cut down rattan, and also to apply for their land title. The influx of Filipinos hunting for land had increased perilously. They agreed they had to have titles to their own land lest they be forced off it and have to leave behind the fruit trees and other plants they had begun to cultivate.

But all these government formalities had to be put aside. We had a patient on our hands. Manindok and Bisi eased Mabilis off Manindok's back. He crumpled into our wicker chair. He had never been robust, but now there was nothing left of him. In haste we laid down our woven mat. They shifted him on to it, and we propped a pillow under his head. "He's coughing and vomiting blood," Manindok said fearfully. "And he can't eat any more."

The doctor in Pinamalayan confirmed Dode's suspicions that Mabilis was a severe case of TB, so we kept him in town with us, asking Lutero, his younger brother, to stay to keep him company. After several weeks of injections, medicine, vitamins, good food, and our morale-building schemes, he got stronger and took an interest in life once more. When he was strong enough to return to the mountains, we explained his sickness to him, telling him that he needed lots of rest. We stressed the prohibitions. Once he was in the mountains, any strenuous work was out. He could not clear land to make a new field. And he must not go on any evangelistic trips until he got back on his feet again.

Our counsel sobered him to discouragement. What was left? He couldn't make a living. He couldn't go out preaching. He could only lie on the floor while everybody else worked in the fields or enjoyed good fun damming off the river for a big catch of fish. He returned to his mountains heavy of heart.

Several days later Dode and I joined them all again. By that time Mabilis had turned into a morose young man, with no interest in anything. His books stayed stowed in their plastic bag, his writing materials untouched. No matter how hard we tried, we couldn't get his face to break into one of his cheerful smiles. He improved through the weeks, however, and got strong enough to walk out to the sweet potato patch to pick some green leaves for a vegetable dinner. He did it mechanically, brooding.

We knew it was more than his health that worried him. Throughout the day whenever Atla burst into the house, his eyes followed her, beseeching some sign of reassurance. But Atla stole only occasional glances at him. No doubt she was weighing the matter that was most important to all tribal girls: what good was a husband who couldn't work? We guessed that he felt her misgivings. It was a struggle, and we watched as God temporarily risked His name to make His man.

Manindok was being tested too. His two-year-old son Samuel, a cranky mama's boy, was sick, and had been sick for some time. No medicine of ours helped him and he got progressively worse, as did his disposition. One day Manindok pushed his way through the leaves hung in the doorway to keep the rain out, carrying Samuel in his arms.

"Will you pray for him?" he pleaded. "He's not getting any better. We're afraid he's going to die." Samuel was a pitiable sight. We agreed to pray, but before we had a chance to bow our heads, Manindok said, "There's something I should tell you before you pray. It's something you don't know about." We relaxed against the wall listening to his explanation.

"Many years ago, before I believed Our Father, I was cursed by one of the men on our mountain. He pronounced the curse that none of my children would ever grow up. And that curse came into effect. We have lost nine children. You remember the girl that died just after you got back last year?" We nodded, remembering her swollen tummy and bulging eyes that stared at everybody, unseeing. She was about four when she died. "She was the ninth one," he added.

Manindok looked down at Samuel. "He's all we've got left," he said, "so will you ask Our Father to make him well again?"

We called everybody together immediately and prayed. We didn't merely pray for healing, but for deliverance from the power of the demons who had made life so miserable for this couple.

Samuel got worse instead of better, and everybody accepted the inevitable, that Samuel wouldn't be with us much longer. We felt it would be hard for Manindok to accept the fact that, while God always hears us when we pray, He doesn't always answer in the way that we want Him to. When we asked Manindok about it, he paused for a minute, collecting his thoughts, and then replied quietly, "Well, if Samuel dies, we know that it'll be Our Father who takes him and not the demons." His wife, who had recently asked for baptism along with twelve others, followed his example of faith; and though she often looked longingly at the little fellow as he lay in her lap exhausted with fever and pain, she managed to smile in spite of it.

Pedro couldn't smile over his problems. The whisperers told us that his wife kept nagging him to perform the old ceremonies to appease the demons. The framework of our Tadyawan church was tottering. All five members were suffering in temptation: Mabilis with his sickness, Manindok with his dying son, Pedro with his heathen wife, Lutero with no prospects of finding a Christian wife, and Bisi with Atla's innocent flirtation, for during those dark days of uncertainty, she found Bisi, though now married, a good match for her wit. Strong and firm in many of the principles of God, Bisi was nevertheless weak in resisting feminine charms. In addition, the congregation as a whole, now numbering about sixty, was going through severe testing, and we with them. We prayed, we wept, we worried. But we couldn't see our way through the problem. We believed Romans 8.28: "All things work together for good to them that love God." We felt sure that everything would work out in the end. But in the meantime? We prayed and wept and worried some more until one day the Lord corrected our thinking. We had been saying that everything would work out all right eventually, but He said to us, "Everything is all right even now. The problem has progressed to the exact stage that I intended for today. Everything works together, not eventually, but is working together even right now, for good."

It was something we all needed to remember too when Sokponsyo walked into our lives. He was a Tawbuid from the mountains two days' walk away. One Saturday morning when Dode was away on vacation, I was sitting on a log in the quiet of an overgrown field preparing the Sunday messages, and if I hadn't looked up when I did, I wouldn't have seen him, for his trained feet picked their way carefully and never made a sound. Ashes and soot completely covered his brown body, bent slightly as he stealthily made his way through the field, head turning from side to side as if anticipating attack from an enemy. I didn't move—just watched. He made his way all across the field until he reached the edge. I lost sight of him then, but hearing a dog snarl and a sharp voice shouting the dog down, I knew Sokponsyo had arrived at the house. I went on with my preparation.

By the time I got back to the house, everybody else had come home, and the house was humming with conversation. In the middle of things sat Sokponsyo listening intently to what first one, and then another taught him from the Word of God. Mabilis perked up and entered right into things too. Pedro slipped away from the crowd and came over to where I was filling up a basin of water to wash my face. "He's come to hear the teaching," he said excitedly, and sucked through his teeth several times. "He likes what he's heard so far. We must pray now so that he'll receive it." And he started to scuttle back across the floor.

"Where did he come from, and how did he know we all lived here?" I asked, detaining him.

"We don't know him very well," he said hurriedly. "But he had heard of us and the teaching. Tawbuid in the interior told him about it. He has come here because of a dream." And with that, not waiting for further questions from me, he whizzed around on his haunches and shuffled back to the group. I heard Sokponsyo say, "This is good teaching; I'd like to hear more."

The Tadyawan didn't fail him. Before supper, after supper, and on into the night they taught him, earnestly, convincingly, beseechingly. And on into the night, when most of us had stretched out for sleep, Sokponsyo listened. I pulled my left arm out of my sleeping bag and looked at my watch. It was 3 a.m.

Everybody was drowsy at the Sunday worship service next morning, and the usual sleepers went to sleep sooner than usual. Yet Sokponsyo sat listening all through the service and afterwards when the men took up the teaching from there and went on for several hours more. Only after that did Sokponsyo dare to come near me. Pedro accompanied him and started the conversation. "He says he came here because people in his dream told him he should."

Sokponsyo peered at me through eyes squinting in the smoke of his pipe. "Will you tell me about it?" I asked. Removing his pipe from his charcoaled mouth and placing it beside him on the floor, he haltingly began his story in the best Tadyawan he could muster.

"In my dream I was sitting in a big house with all my friends and relatives, including the elders of our mountain. We were having a great palaver. You two women and your teaching was the subject. Some thought you were good people, while others felt you were evil and that all your teaching was bad. Some insisted that you weren't people at all, but demons whose houses are under the ground. We couldn't agree and began shouting at each other. The elders in the dream then concluded that there was only one way to find out who was right— someone should be sent to see and to hear. In the dream they appointed me, and that's why I came yesterday."

"You were afraid yesterday, weren't you?" I said smiling.

"Yes," and he emphasized it. "But now I see that you are a real person and that your teaching is good. These men have taught me lots, but I'd like to hear more. They say there's lots more to hear. I'm going home tomorrow, but I'll be back." He grabbed his pipe, put it back in the corner of his mouth, and sat there with nothing more to say.

Early the next morning, when our community Bible study was finished, everybody scattered. Remaining in the house to fold up the teaching materials, I heard Sokponsyo's voice carry from the field where he was already making his way back to the home and darkness he had left five days ago. "Pray for me," he called to the Tadyawan outside, "so that I won't be dissuaded by my neighbours. I want to believe."

I gathered my laundry together, jammed it into a pail, and started out for the stream. Pedro stopped me on the way. "What about that dream? I know that lots of the heathen's dreams are from the demons, but that couldn't have been from a demon, could it? The devil wouldn't encourage people to come and hear Our Father's words, would he?"

I had to agree with him.

"We'll have to pray lots for Sokponsyo," he added.

"You don't understand how hard it is for a man to go back to all his people and leaders and say that he wants to follow your teaching."

If ever a man was prayed for, it was Sokponsyo! Somebody was sure to mention his name in prayer at every morning meeting and every evening meeting. Two weeks later, more confident now, Sokponsyo led his own family and four other families across the same field that he had so fearfully crossed previously. The Tadyawan's excitement filled the smoke-stained house. Nobody worked in the fields longer than he had to, for they all wanted to share in teaching these people. Mabilis, because he still had to rest most of the time, took the lead, but others of the men who usually remained shyly in the background, came to the fore and convincingly added their bit. When the five families left to go back home, friendships had been welded, and the hunger for God's Word heightened. "We'll be back to hear more," they said with certainty when they left.

Their response was the most encouraging the Tadyawan church had seen for some time. Evangelism took a new turn after that, and many of the men began making plans for short trips over the mountains to teach their relatives. Mabilis, though still unable to go himself, joined in the enthusiasm, coaching the men and encouraging them. He was gaining strength and often allowed himself to be cheerful, though Atla still worried him.

"Do you think Atla is a believer?" Pedro asked us one day on behalf, we felt, of Mabilis, who was sitting nearby, alert to our conversation.

"We think so," we said, "but that will be for you men to decide when you examine the candidates for baptism, for she is one who has asked to be baptized. We'll sit in with you, though, in case you'd like some advice." He looked relieved.

There was a stir in the air on the afternoon of examinations. Everybody was sent out of the house except the five baptized believers and the two of us. One by one, they called the thirteen in, questioning them and then letting them go, afterwards discussing the person privately among themselves.

"No," spoke up Bisi, "I don't think Sabil should be baptized. She still has visits from the demons. There must be something wrong, because what's-his-name's wife across the river said that when she believed, she no longer had any visits from her wise-one or the demons.

"And Kalobang shouldn't be baptized yet either," chimed in Lutero, "for he often sings the songs that the demons taught him from way back. He says he doesn't mean it, but still he shouldn't do it."

Down the list they went. Kostil couldn't be baptized because there were rumours that she still flirted with her former husband. Bogado couldn't because he didn't even know what believing and being baptized was all about. Dalioman should be deferred because his desire wasn't sincere. He had asked for baptism only because his mother, Sabil, made him do it.

"And Atla?" we interjected. "What do you feel about her?"

Mabilis sat rigid. "I hate to say this," said Manindok, "because she is my niece, but she is a thief. She often steals food from my garden and trees. If she were ready for baptism, she wouldn't steal." Mabilis didn't utter a word, but the other three agreed with Manindok. Atla, along with the other five, would have to be deferred. We felt Mabilis's keen disappointment.

"Now, how should we let these people know they've been deferred?" we asked.

Pedro, quick to understand, spoke up, "I think it would be a good idea if we announced in church our reasons for turning them down. Then everybody will know and nobody will be able to try to guess the reason and start gossiping. And we should tell the congregation not to laugh at them or talk about them, but to pray for them so that they can be baptized the next time."

We raised a question: "Do you think that those deferred should be told privately first before we make a public explanation? If privately, we could encourage them to keep on walking with Our Father and to trust Him for deliverance over the things that are standing in their way."

They agreed. "Who'll tell them, then?" and our eyes shot round at the five. Pedro sucked through his teeth furiously. Mabilis's eyes wandered on walls and roof, falling finally on his feet. Manindok giggled in self-defence. Bisi and Lutero just sat. It was evident nobody wanted that job.

We compromised. "All right, we'll tell the women who were turned down, if you tell the men." They nodded reluctantly. "And we ought to tell them right away to keep the conjecturing from getting out of hand," we continued.

Atla was my assignment. I called her to a private walk to the fields, chasing away the children whose unconquerable inquisitiveness made them follow us. Sitting on a fallen log, we chatted lightly, and then I asked, "Why did you want to be baptized, Atla?"

"Because I now believe in Our Jesus," she replied, picking soil from around her finger nails.

"You really do believe in Him, do you?" I probed.

"Yes," she answered, cocking her head and giving me a quick look. "I don't follow any of the demon ways any more."

"But when we believe in Jesus, He gives us new life. Are you still living in the old life?"

"I've left the old life," she asserted, "all of it."

"But what about your stealing, Atla? The others say you still steal, little things like fruit and vegetables. Is that true?"

She pouted and then hung her head. "Yes," she admitted quietly, "sometimes when I'm walking through a field and get hungry, I take whatever is ripe for eating, no matter whose field it is."

"It's because of that, Atla, that the believers feel you should be deferred for baptism. We'll all be praying for you that you will get strength to overcome that temptation." She smiled weakly and said she would pray too.

Some time later Dode and I were outside the house, chopping kindling for our fireplace, when Pedro and Mabilis approached us. "Do you think Atla believes Our Father's words even though she steals?" Pedro asked.

"Yes, she is a believer," we said. Mabilis smiled.

20 Helpmeet for Mabilis

"Here," and Atla shoved a tiny scrap of paper into our hands, smiling so broadly that her black eyes were only slits above her chubby cheeks. Merriment in the voices outside the house indicated that everybody knew what the note was about. No doubt they had all helped her to read it just after Mabilis had given it to her. Now she wanted us to read it.

"From Mabilis. Atla, I want you if you want me. But I don't want you if you don't want me."

We looked at her. The bashful miss was twirling her fingers in and around her loosely hanging cloak, which was a flour sack, vivid printing still on it, slit down one side and tied over one shoulder. It was her only clothing except the usual G-string.

"How are you going to answer it?" we inquired, putting aside the sugar cane we were chewing, anticipating a nice sisterly chat. Instead Atla made a mad leap for one of the upright poles in the house and hid her face behind it. Giggling weakly, she answered, "I don't know." Then her whole body took refuge behind the pole. There was a long silence.

Dode and I picked up our sugar cane again. "Dode," I questioned, "did you hear what Pedro said this morning about Sokponsyo?"

Dode shook her head. "He says," I went on to explain, "that he's just found out why we haven't seen Sokponsyo and the other families. They've been cursed. When they returned to their area from their visit here, the elder was exceedingly angry and put a curse on them, saying that if ever they came our way again to listen to the teaching, they would all die."

"Who told Pedro?" asked Dode, reaching for another piece of sugar cane.

"One of our men who was on an evangelistic trip met some of Sokponsyo's friends. When he tried to teach them, they warded him off with the news of Sokponsyo and the curse. Pedro seems stunned by it all. He's so positive that the Lord had given the dream in the first place that he can't understand how the devil could get in so fast and spoil it. Even more confusing to him is that the Lord doesn't give Sokponsyo another dream, telling him that he doesn't have to worry about the curse and that he should come anyway. And, who knows, maybe the Lord will do just that. Did you notice at prayers this morning that Pedro asked the Lord to give Sokponsyo another dream? That's what was behind it all."

Atla, no longer the centre of attention, came over and sat on the floor close by us, fondling the piece of paper, trying to get out the creases with her fingernail. We went on enjoying our sugar cane. Finally she blurted out, "I can't write," and then a flood of embarrassed giggles rushed out.

"We can write the answer for you, if you want," we said as casually as we could. She fidgeted closer but remained silent. Accepting this as her approval of our suggestion, we said, "What shall we write?"

"I don't know," and she bent forward, letting her head fall, bouncing against her knee and then springing back again. A little colour rose in her cheeks. There was another long pause. We snapped off another chew of cane. "Want some sugar cane?" we asked her. She refused it. At that moment there was a howl from the other house.

"He's getting worse," explained Atla, jerking her head in the direction of Samuel's house. "His arm is paralysed now and only one side of his face moves. Manindok and his wife think that he'll die soon. They still pray though, and are not angry with Our Father." And again she looked down at the paper in her lap.

"Do you really want Mabilis for a husband?" we asked without even looking at her.

"Yes," she answered giddily.

"Shall we write that for you then?" We heard a weak "yes" through her giggles and acted promptly. We handed the finished note to her and, with a bounce, she was up and out of the house, detained momentarily by her cape which caught on to a branch in the doorway, exposing her sturdy body. She threw her head back, loudly laughing, and then unhooked the cape from the branch, ran down the pole-stair, leaped on to the ground and raced off.

Feeling that the romance had progressed far enough for the church to take some action, we asked some of the baptized members about it. "Do you think we should get together to discuss whether or not they should be allowed to take their vows before Our Father?" we asked.

"Not quite," they advised. "You two should talk with them together to see if they really mean it. If you hear it from their own mouths, then we'll know it's true that they want each other."

Dode and I waited for the auspicious moment when others weren't in the house, and then told Mabilis and Atla that we'd like to see them both. Atla sat at one end of the house, while Mabilis fiddled in the fireplace at the other end. Dode and I sat in the middle, turning our heads first to one and then to the other as we asked questions that we thought would reveal their feelings, about whether it was the Lord's will for them to marry.

"Mabilis," we ventured, "can you see any reason why Atla shouldn't be your wife?" He jerked his knees up under his chin and stared hard into the dying embers.

"Only one," he said. "I'm gaining my health back now, but suppose I would get seriously ill again. I wonder if she'd be tempted to leave me to find another husband who would be able to provide for her."

"What about it?" we turned to Atla. "Your vows before Our Father would be binding."

She glanced away from us, toyed with her fingernails, and then said timidly, "No, I won't leave him. I will not look for another."

The church was satisfied with our report. "We're ready to discuss it now," they said, "to see if we all agree to this marriage."

Mabilis and Atla squirmed under the scrutiny of the five members of the church when we gathered one bright morning. The church probed sincerely, feeling their responsibility in anything that was connected with Our Father.

"Mabilis," asked Pedro, "what if Our Father doesn't give Atla any children, will you hunt for another wife?" Mabilis assured them that he wouldn't.

"But what if Our Father gives you children, will you teach them about Him?" They both were emphatic in their "yes".

"Mabilis," interjected Manindok, "what about Atla's stealing? Are you going to help her, and will you pray with her for deliverance?"

Before Mabilis had a chance to answer, Sabil listening in at the window shouted out indignantly, "But she won't steal any more once she's married, for then she'll have a field of her own." And then as if to explain to Dode and me, she turned to us and shouted through the window, "Young girls steal only from other fields until they get their own, then they don't have to any more." Grunts of agreement went round the house. Mabilis promised, though, to help her.

Practical Bisi shot a quick question at Atla. "Atla, Mabilis is a very good teacher of Our Father's words. What will you do if Our Father asks him to go on an evangelistic trip? Will you hinder Mabilis from going on it? Will you tell him you'll be too sad and lonely?"

Atla caught a little breath, blinked her eyes, and then almost whispered, "I will not stop him from going." And with that the church gave their approval for these two to exchange their vows before Our Father, saying, "You can be married any time you like."

They chose a busy Sunday for their wedding day. We had had a morning worship service and a baptismal service for the seven accepted candidates, and then the Lord's Supper for all twelve members of the Tadyawan church. Only the sheer joy of it all kept Dode and me from being exhausted. We were just beginning to catch our breath when Mabilis approached us. "We'd like to be married today after the afternoon meeting." It left us in a dither. Mabilis and Atla were as ready for their wedding as they'd ever be, for no fashion code demanded a wedding dress or groom's tail coat, but we needed to get the ceremony together! With no time for anything else, we decided to use the same ceremony we had used for Bisi and Kasosok's wedding.

That afternoon during the church service we announced that Mabilis and Atla would be married as soon as the meeting was over. Everybody stayed, and we had a difficult time reshuffling folk so that enough floor space was cleared for the couple to sit at least somewhere near each other. Without ever glancing in each other's direction they quietly exchanged vows, making their promise to Our Father, "until death us do part". Then we turned to the congregation.

"You have all heard their vows, do you all promise before Our Father that you will not try in any way to entice them from each other?" They promised.

"And do you promise to rout anybody from the area who would come in for that purpose?" Again they strongly assented. Mabilis and Atla were now man and wife. It had been a long wait for Mabilis, but the wait was worth it, for the Lord had given him a devoted wife and helpmeet, as the years ahead were to prove.

21 The Church Grows Up

It was the crack of dawn. Roosters were crowing and the chickens fluttering to the ground. Inside our tribal house things were already astir. Fires crackled under blackened pots of either rice or sweet potatoes, while the Tadyawan, huddled near their fireplaces to warm up after a chilly night, conversed in subdued tones. Only the small children were allowed the luxury of an extra forty winks.

Dode and I had rolled up our sleeping bags and were keeping a sleepy eye on our pot of rice dangling from a metal hook over the fire we shared with Mapol's family. Mapol himself was squatting as close to the fire as he dared get without being singed, while his demure wife sat nearby, bent over a piece of paper she was writing on in the light of the fire. Still sound asleep and tightly wrapped up in their blankets, their two children were curled up against the wall. Mapol's wife reached for Mapol's already-folded blanket and threw it over the children.

When all the water had boiled off our rice, our eyes searched the walls and roof for a rattan lid-lifter. Mapol, sensing what we wanted, stretched out his hand, and, bare-fingered, removed the hot iron lid from the kettle, waited for us to put the slices of cheese on top, and then put the lid back on. Separating the logs to reduce the heat, we left the rice to cook its last few minutes in its own steam. Mapol's wife moved closer to the fire, bent forward still more, and squinted at her paper in the light of the dying fire.

When our breakfast was cooked, we nodded to Mapol. In a second he reassembled the logs, blew several times on the hot ends of them, and had the fire blazing again. His wife straightened her back and stopped squinting as she went on writing. By the time their potatoes were boiled, she had finished writing and had tucked her paper in one of her books. It was time to awaken the children, a job that called for a stern command to get up. Little Elizabeth fretted and kicked her objections against the wall, while drowsy, fat-tummied Benjamin staggered over to the fire and leaned heavily against his dad. Mapol gave him a fatherly hug. Mapol's wife, in an effort to get Benjamin fully awake, grabbed her note from her book and, with a determined pat on their son's bare seat, said, "Here, give this to the two sisters."

The writing wasn't the best, but in the semi-dark house we could make out the words, "We are going to build a house for Our Father." It was the first inkling we had had that they were thinking of building a church. We tried our best to conceal our excitement, fearing that Mapol's wife, following her usual bent, was giving away a group secret.

It wasn't a secret, however, for after the morning meeting, the loud conversation outside the house was of cogon grass for the roof, bamboo for the floor, and trees for the foundation poles. We knew then that it was really happening. "Just imagine," we marvelled to each other, "a real church building instead of meeting here in the house!" Having never felt at liberty to suggest it ourselves, we had prayed about it often. Now we couldn't get over their taking complete initiative!

Panot was the first to tell us another surprise later in the day as he paused outside to rest from his heavy burden of cogon. "We're thinking of putting a room at the back end of the church for you two to live in." A "parsonage"! It was like icing on the cake. We dared only a cautious elation lest the plan never materialize.

Our doubts, however, were unfounded. After we had gone back to town, they finished the church and the parsonage and then got everything in readiness for our return, even moving our old tin trunk and the water pails into the parsonage for us. Accompanying us back into their mountains for our next stay with them, they led us with quiet pride to the clearing where the big church stood out neat and clean, encircled by several smaller houses for individual families. The children were gaily playing on the ground under the church building when we arrived, and the adults, who had picked up our voices coming up the mountain trail, were on hand, watching us with eager eyes so as not to miss our joyous reaction. We didn't disappoint them, and for once we could let our enthusiasm carry us away as we examined church and parsonage.

The building was a credit to their imagination, for it was spacious, with a roof high enough for us to stand upright in every corner, in contrast to their houses, where standing room was limited to the centre of the house, with the roof slanting down to meet walls two feet high. To one side of the church room there was a big fireplace, where, they explained, we could do our cooking and where they could keep warm on cool mornings or evenings during the services. They were proud of their new church and the small parsonage attached, and we were too.

During the building of the church, when not only the baptized ones but the whole congregation pitched in, one thing became apparent to them and to us too. "We're not organized," they complained, "and everybody just does what he wants to do; so we have too many people off hunting for bamboo and not enough getting the cogon for the roof."

At another stage they remarked, "We Tadyawan are used to following a leader. We need somebody to co-ordinate things; otherwise, either everybody tries to tell everybody else what to do or else nobody will make any decision." We knew then it was time for some informal church organization.

Following the dedication of the church one gorgeous Sunday in September, 1965, we broached the subject of appointing several men, perhaps three to begin with, to be in charge of practical matters in the church, such as overseeing the care of church property and grounds and having things in readiness for Communion Sunday, and baptism Sunday when a stream had to be dammed off to provide a big enough pool. When the congregation agreed, we surprised them by saying that they were the ones to choose the three men. It was a new idea to them. Formerly in Tadyawan culture a leader rose with an automatic following according to the extent of power his wise-one invested in him, and his followers complied with his wishes unquestioningly in exchange for the benefits of his healing and prophetic powers. But now to have to choose leaders from among themselves to be co-ordinators in practical matters left them nonplussed. They confessed they had no idea what significant qualifications they should look for.

We named a few. Since it would be recognized as a position in the church, the job should be filled only by baptized believers, and the co-ordinators should not be too shy to tell others what to do, nor too domineering, and open to the opinions of others.

"Well then," Panot interrupted, "if only the baptized ones qualify for this job, I suggest that only the ones not baptized choose. In that way we'll be sure to have everybody's support when there's work to be done." It was a good idea, and everybody agreed to carry it through—with one exception. Recommendations could come from anybody in the congregation, baptized or not.

When the floor was open for suggestions, however, nobody would say a thing. They all just sat there, looking at each other or staring at us. Even when we exhorted them to overcome their shyness and graciously to speak their minds, still they sat, wriggling from one position to another or whispering among themselves. Fearing that we'd be there for the rest of the afternoon, we decided to call on some individuals. "Pedro, what about you? What three men do you think would be able to handle the job?"

Pedro looked frightened at being singled out and said abruptly, "Not me, I don't know." And with that he excused himself by becoming earnestly solicitous of his son's runny nose.

"Bisi, you, any ideas?" His boyhood shyness overcame him, and he was speechless. Encouraged that he didn't say "no", however, we tried to get some word out of him. "What three would you like to see elected as co-ordinators?"

Slowly he lifted his chin from off the bright red, unmended sweater he was wearing above his G-string and haltingly spoke in the silence of the church building, "The three I want are . . . Mabilis . . . and Panot . . . and . . . ." He stopped right there.

"Who else?" we asked. "That's two; what's your third choice?"

"I don't know," and with an awkward smile Bisi let his chin fall back on his chest again.

His tribal modesty was hilarious to us, though we didn't dare let it show. His third choice was obviously himself! Others must have agreed with the tacit nomination of himself, for after further suggestions and discussion, Bisi got his wish and was elected along with Mabilis and Panot. All three were young men, earnest in the things of God and with evident gifts of leadership and teaching. Dode and I hoped that someday they would attend the tribal Bible school, which had just completed its first year.

The Tadyawan had been introduced to the Bible school when the school was still in the making. Sessions were to be held in the high, cold mountains of the Alangan tribe; but since there was a great deal of work attached to getting classrooms and student houses built, the Alangan sent out a plea to all the tribal churches for help.

When the plea first came, we hoped that some of the Tadyawan would want to go, though Alangan country was far north of us and would involve considerable travel expense. When we announced, however, to the Tadyawan church the Alangan's need for help, Bisi and Pedro responded immediately. "Do you mean that tribes from all over the island will be there?" they inquired bright-eyed.

"Yes," we assured them. "Christians from the Alangan, Iraya, Buhid, Hanunoo and Tawbuid will all be there to help."

"Kiiiiiii," shouted Bisi, overwhelmed with the thought of tribesmen having fellowship with former rivals. Pedro's eyes got big, and he clamped his mouth tightly shut with a "hmmmm". Then, not being able to contain his amazement, he jerked his head around toward us and asked, "You mean we'll be seeing our brothers and sisters, those who listen to Our Father's words, all from different tribes?"

Bisi's and Pedro's enthusiasm was catching, and soon eight men were figuring out how they could earn enough money for the bus fare to the northern part of the island. Once they decided what to sell, the whole house turned into action. Some dried rice either in the sun or in huge black frying pans over the fire; others went off to the fields to collect vegetables or fruit; while still others spent every spare minute making rattan swings. Wives pitched in to help too, and while the men made new handles for their jungle knives, the women mended old, discoloured blankets or applied needle, thread, and ingenuity to well-worn travel trousers.

The whole expedition was a grand success, and the men came back telling us of all they had accomplished, and boasting of their new friends from all over the island. "And at the Sunday meeting they took a collection," Marcos told us. "We didn't know anything about that, but they explained it to us. They give that money to Our Father."

"We could start taking collections in our services too," we interrupted, not wanting to miss this golden opportunity. And from then on, on the first Sunday after the full moon of every month, the people dropped, some with more ostentation than others, their coins or paper money into the glass peanut butter jar that was passed around. They had agreed among themselves that five *centavos* for each Sunday was the right amount, making their offering twenty *centavos* per month, and they held to it as if it were a business deal.

One Sunday when we started the jar on its journey and the people were still digging into their bits of rag tied securely around their coins, Bisi shouted over to his sister, "Hey, Dolilaw, you owe Our Father forty *centavos* this month because you didn't give Him anything last month." Dolilaw dug further into her rag and paid her debt, while Dode and I enjoyed the amusing irreverence.

With the new church, however, we felt it was time for some new giving, giving that would be meaningful and worshipful. Their business arrangement was fine for a start, but they had missed the whole point of giving to the Lord; for after a year, no matter how many new flashlights, mirrors, gaudy T-shirts, or tins of sardines they bought when they sold their rattan or worked in a Filipino's field, they still gave the Lord only His prescribed five *centavos.*

"You see," we exhorted them during a morning meeting, "you have bought lots of things for yourselves with the money you've earned from working or selling rattan, but you keep most of it to buy things you want. You give very little to Our Father for His work. How will others hear that Our Jesus died for their sins unless the evangelists go to tell them? And the evangelists need money for the bus fare and food." Then we presented the idea of tithing.

The arithmetic stumped them. While most had learned to add up their purchases and then count their change at the town stores, it was still difficult for some. One man avoided the problem of addition by buying one item at a time. But now we were asking them to figure out what a tenth was! They looked completely bewildered.

"It's not hard to figure out," we encouraged. "There are ten ten-*centavo* pieces in every peso; so out of every *peso* that you earn, one ten-*centavo* piece belongs to Our Father. If you earn two *pesos*, then two ten-*centavo* pieces are His. Or if you harvest ten sacks of rice, one sack should be given to Him."

Then to test their comprehension, we gave them an example to figure out: "If you got ten *pesos* for selling bananas, how much would you give to Our Father?"

The women looked mystified, but the men held their

fingers in front of their faces, their lips moving as they counted off. "One *peso*," shouted Panot.

"No," yelled Pedro; but when he noted our nod of approval to Panot, he quickly corrected himself, "Yes, that's right, one *peso*." Then sitting huddled together in little groups, they discussed the idea and concluded that they would like to give the tenth to Our Father. A real quiz followed as they teased each other in trying to figure out the tenth.

Panot never lost an opportunity for a joke, and he had one on this occasion. "What do we give Our Father when there is a litter of only five pigs?" he called to us above the din. With that he caught everybody's attention, and all the buzzing stopped so that they could hear the answer to the puzzle.

"Well," we announced, with twinkles in our eyes, "when the piglets grow up, you could sell one of them and give half the price to Our Father."

Panot, with astonished eyes, threw back his head, slapped his thigh, and laughingly exclaimed, "Well, that's a good one. I wondered what good half a piglet would do Him. It'd just be waste to cut it up." And he gave Mabilis a friendly punch on the arm. Mabilis tittered and nudged Atla in the ribs. The meeting was over for the day, and they went outside to have a tug-of-war.

22 An Attempt to Free Pidyong

Even though it was a dull, damp Sunday morning, we knew we'd have full-house at church that day because we were expecting some of the evangelists to be back. Ever since the church had begun to give more liberally, the evangelists accepted our challenge to a more intensive evangelistic thrust. Leaving their families and fields for several days, they trekked over Eastern Mindoro's mountains, sometimes alone, sometimes in groups of two or three—Pedro, Mabilis, Kalobang, Dalioman, Panot, Bisi, Manindok, Poyo and others. But they always came back with the same sorrowful, seemingly hopeless report. This Sunday's was no exception. "Bilbino stands in the way of our preaching," they proclaimed in defeated tones at the morning meeting. "Whenever we're questioned and have to admit that he doesn't believe, they won't listen to us any more. They think we're rascals for side-stepping Bilbino."

"And besides Bilbino's being a barrier," chimed in Mabilis, "we've got to pray that leaders in other areas will believe, because if they don't, then neither will their people. All groups are afraid of the power their leaders have. If a leader doesn't want the gospel, he'll curse his people who do want to hear it."

"Like Sokponsyo," I commented.

"Yes," they agreed; and then someone added, "By the way, did anybody tell you he's dead?"

I was momentarily stunned by the news. "Where did you hear that?" I blurted out, not wanting to believe what I had heard.

"I met a cousin of his the other day when I was getting some cogon grass to repair my roof, and he told me. I asked him how he died, and he said it was probably the flu."

While they talked among themselves after that, I sat quietly with my own thoughts. I wondered if it really *was* the flu that took Sokponsyo's life or if he, daring to express a continued interest in the gospel, was cursed after all or even poisoned. Demonically controlled leaders, we had learned, stopped at nothing to maintain their own power and interests.

A painful cry from Samuel interrupted my conjecturings. "It won't be long now," someone from the congregation pitifully announced. I shot a glance in the direction of the cry. Manindok and his wife, sitting close together on the floor, were looking down at the grey little skeleton of their son lying on some rags in her lap. She slowly raised her head and looked at us despairingly, her tired, hopeless eyes searching our faces. Her hands reached for his little body, and she turned him over. Wearily looking at us again, and without any words, she pointed to nodules on Samuel's spine. Wide-eyed, Dode and I looked at each other. It was the first significant symptom we had seen. Samuel had TB of the spine! Dode wasted no time in starting him on INH, the prescribed medication for TB. She wondered, however, how effective it would be at such an advanced stage, for he was already paralysed, his mother told us, all down his right side.

After we had a time of prayer for Samuel, Kalobang brought us back to our original subject. "What Mabilis said earlier is true. Praying for the conversion of leaders *is* the right thing to do." Scratching the sole of his foot, he continued, "Remember my cousin at Tigaw on the Pola River who wanted to believe? Even though he liked the teaching, he couldn't go over the head of his leader. It was too big a risk to take. Being cursed is no joke. His leader has forbidden them all to listen to our teaching."

"And surely that's what's wrong with Pidyong," broke in Pedro. "He's never admitted that he's afraid of his leader, but that's what it amounts to." With disappointed overtones, everybody grunted in agreement. They had been following the happenings in Pidyong's area with much interest and prayer, and the outcome discouraged them all.

Months previously, Pedro and Manindok had gone north to Pasi to teach the gospel to the people there. It had been hard going, for many of the people had turned them away with contempt, despising their teaching altogether. But in one small section of that large area they met Pidyong, a leader over four families, but himself under greater authority. Pidyong was genuinely interested in the Word of God, declaring to the two men, "It doesn't matter if my wife believes, or my people believe, or my leader believes, this is what I want, and this is what I'm going to follow." Pedro and Manindok were jubilant and decided to leave the phonograph and gospel records with Pidyong so that he could listen to the teaching all he wanted until they could get back to visit him again.

The Tadyawan church received the news concerning Pidyong with great enthusiasm, and from that day on, both publicly and privately, the families began to pray for Pidyong, some with more fervency than others. Atla got carried away in her prayers for him—at one morning meeting, she asked the Lord to "protect Our Pidyong from 'Our Devil'." There were a few titters from the bowed heads of the congregation. Atla spluttered, then recovered herself and re-worded her prayer, "Protect our Pidyong from our enemy, the devil." How to use these names *did* present problems to the Tadyawan!

Atla's prayer, however, was an appropriate one, for although none of us fully realized at the time how desperate a struggle we would engage in against the powers of darkness, we knew there would be conflict.

The conflict became apparent about three weeks later. All unsuspecting, Pidyong's leader, with a small delegation of his own people, came down to our area and visited one of the families who lived about half an hour's walk away from the church. In his possession Anggalong, the leader, carried the phonograph the men had given to Pidyong. It was obvious to the family that Anggalong was angry, and they sent off one of their small sons to alert the rest of the men so that they would come for moral support.

"Take this phonograph back," shouted Anggalong. "Don't give it to Pidyong any more. He can't have it. Every time he plays the phonograph a multitude of demons comes up out of the ground and lurks in our area. There are more demons now than we ever had. Everybody has noticed it, and we don't like it. We've had enough demons to deal with. The leader over me, that powerful one in the interior, has heard about it too, and he says he'll curse us all if we don't get rid of the phonograph."

Our people tried to pacify him. "And furthermore," Anggalong shouted authoritatively, "none of you can come into my area again to teach. If you've got relatives there, you can visit them, but you can't teach them. We don't want your teaching in our area; so don't come." This was a blow to the Tadyawan, and to us too when they told us about it later.

"What did you say when he said that to you?" we asked.

"We told him," explained Panot, "that we couldn't stop teaching even if he commanded it, because the last thing Our Jesus said was to go and tell everybody that He died for them so that they wouldn't have to be punished for their sin." He paused a moment, rubbing his hand down the side of his face, then wrinkled up his nose and added, "But even if we said that to him, there's not much sense in trying to evangelize in his area. Who would be brave enough to listen? They'd probably all run away."

The church was low in spirit for some time after this, being concerned for Pidyong, one lone man in forbidden territory. Often we sat around after church chatting over the problem and trying to figure out some way to get around the prohibition. But there seemed no way until one morning Mabilis inspired us all with his thought. "But Anggalong hasn't forbidden you two women to go in to teach in his area. We couldn't guide you in, but if you went in by yourselves and taught, he wouldn't stop you because he knows that this is your work, like that of the priests in town."

Everybody straightened up with hearty approval. Dode and I agreed to the job, but one hindrance loomed on the horizon of our thinking: how would we find the place? We didn't know our way around the depths of the forest in Pidyong's area. When we mentioned our reservations to the Tadyawan they shouted us down with assurances that it was easy, eagerly adding helpful directions, all about certain forks in the trail or certain trees as landmarks or particular plants. Our heads swam. Pedro, seeing our consternation, asked for a piece of paper and with stiff fingers tried to draw us a map. We still looked doubtful. To both Dode and me, born in well-mapped-out cities, the forest had a way of looking the same no matter where we were. Trails were often no wider than ten inches and entrances to them so obscured at times that unsuspecting people could stand right in front of them and not see them. Dolilaw saw our reluctance to take on unfamiliar forest without Tadyawan guides. "We'll pray for you," she soothed. "And if you get lost, just turn around and come back out the same way you went in."

Her advice was cold comfort.

We made two attempts, however, at getting there, using Pedro's map; but each time we went in circles at the very spot where his map said we should descend the mountain. We tried many a little trail but were led nowhere. Huge blisters on our feet and nightfall compelled us to return to town both times.

How the Tadyawan laughed at our forest ignorance when we told them about our unfruitful efforts! It *was* funny except that we still hadn't solved our problem of getting to Pidyong.

A few weeks later in a casual and unexpected way the answer came. We wondered why we hadn't thought of it before. We had begun holding language classes in the church building for those who wanted to learn Tagalog, the national language of the Philippines, so that they could soon attend the Bible school. More than prospective students for Bible school attended our classes, however, and they were learning fast. After Tagalog class one day taciturn Marcos stopped us and in as few words as possible told us he wouldn't be attending classes the next few days as he was going to travel up north to look over the plants and fruit trees on his old farmland in Pasi. We connected only one name with Pasi— Pidyong. Knowing, however, that Pasi covered a wide area, we asked Marcos if his fields were near Pidyong's place.

"Not very near," he replied, "but I have to go past his place to get to my fields."

"Will you stop in, then, to see if he's home, and tell him that we want to come in to teach him, but we can't find the right trail. Tell him that we could meet him at the marketplace in the town at the foot of their mountains, and that we could arrange at that time for him to show us the right turn-off. If he likes the idea, tell him to choose the day he wants, and we'll be there. Be sure to tell him to make himself known to us because we don't know him, and lots of Tadyawan are coming out to that marketplace now."

Marcos, in spite of uneasiness and fear of repercussions, carried out the plan; and on the day chosen by Pidyong, Dode and I went to the market to meet the much-prayed-for man and to arrange a time for us to visit his people and teach them. He promised to meet us at the fork in the trail to show us the tricky turn-off three days later. On the appointed day, Dode and I boarded the bus out of Pinamalayan, and rode to the foot of Pidyong's mountains. Climbing a weary climb up the logging road, exposed to the tropical sun, and then over a cooler, more sheltered trail, we arrived at the mountain's crest and the fork in the trail where Pidyong was supposed to meet us, but Pidyong wasn't there. This was as far as we had got before with Pedro's map. We were hot and hungry, and faith began to shrivel. Digging into our army packs, we pulled out our lunch bags and sat beside the deserted trail on this lonely mountain top and began eating. Between bites of cheese sandwiches and gulps of *kalamansi* juice from our water bottle, we noticed on the opposite side of the trail a branch that had been erected perpendicularly. All of its twigs had been cut off except one, which very obviously pointed to the southwest.

Reaching for the cookies, Dode looked thoughtful, "Do you suppose Pidyong could have put that stick there for us?"

"Yes, he could have," I agreed. "Maybe things got too precarious there at his place and he feared being seen with us. Let's chance it and, as soon as we've finished eating, follow the sign. We've got nothing to lose."

Leaving our crumbs behind for an ant feast, we pushed our way through an overgrown trail that lay in the direction of the stick. The trail led us to another not quite so overgrown, and following it for a few yards, we stumbled on to a wide trail leading straight down the mountain side. We felt sure that this was the trail Pedro tried to route us on. Light feet took us down, sometimes through slippery mud, sometimes in stair-step fashion with only the exposed roots of the huge trees to keep our feet in position. Sometimes we missed the roots and with a thud slid on the seat of our "pedal-pushers" a short distance further down the descent. After travelling down several hundred feet, we could hear, in the noiselessness of the mountain ranges, the flow of the river below that Pedro had mapped out. We knew we were on the right trail this time.

The cool freshness of the river revived us. Sitting on its rocks, we removed our shoes, scooped out the gory leeches from between our toes, and let the clear water gush past our feet and legs. Then, after washing the mud off us and off the seats of our "pedal-pushers", we crossed the river and looked for a trail on the other side, which, according to Pedro's directions, should have led us right to Pidyong's settlement. But we could spot no path in that immediate vicinity. Starting to despair, we happened to glance upriver and saw a tribesman grabbing for shrimp under the rocks on the river's edge. We called to him and, encouraged that he didn't run away, we started upriver, at the same time asking him if he knew Pidyong and where he lived. He called back that he knew him and that he'd take us there. Our thrill at being guided right to

Pidyong's door was chilled when we discovered that our guide was Anggalong's brother!

Arriving at Pidyong's area, we found no friendly welcome. Four grass huts housed four families who peered at us, fear and suspicion evident in their eyes. Even Pidyong was aloof. Sensing their fear was of Anggalong's brother, we made no mention of our previous visit to the market nor of the stick we had seen on the trail earlier that morning. When Pidyong found an opportunity later, however, he got near to us and warily looking around asked us if we had seen his sign. "The government land surveyors from town came in early today and made us all work for them," he explained. "I had to help carry in some of their equipment so couldn't come out to meet you. I went off early this morning to make that sign for you. I was hoping you'd see it." It was the only interest or friendliness he dared show at the time.

Even after Anggalong's brother had gone home for the night Pidyong and all his people still seemed apprehensive. Sitting around Pidyong's fireplace, though, they listened to the Bible stories on the mighty power of our great God—power that could keep them from demons and men. We left the next day, hiding our own misgivings by cheerily stating that we'd come back again sometime.

On subsequent visits the people responded more warmly and soon were learning from the Word of God. Though Anggalong's threats hung over their heads, they always said we could come back again to teach them, and they were eager to know all that Our Father said, though they firmly refused to commit themselves personally to the claims of Jesus Christ. Pidyong, nevertheless, became more assertive before his own people in his favour of the gospel. We overheard him talking to a widower one day,

"But these women have come here to show us the way to heaven, just like I did that morning I told you about when I secretly put up that sign to show them where the trail was. I showed them the way, but it was up to them to go that way. Now they are showing us the path to heaven, and it's up to us to follow that path." Even Pidyong's wife told us on one visit, "We don't sacrifice to the demons any more when we're sick; we just pray to Our Father to heal us like you told us to do."

All this good news made the Tadyawan church on the Bansod more bold too. "The next time you go in to Pasi, go and see Anggalong," they commissioned us, "and ask him if he'll change his mind about our coming into his area. We know our own relatives would like to hear the teaching."

We told Pidyong what the Tadyawan church had said. "Sure, go and see Anggalong," he encouraged us, "and when you do, ask him if you can come in here for longer visits. We can't learn much when you come in for only a night or two, and it's hard for us to remember what you do teach us. It would be better if you could come more often and for a longer period of time." We agreed to petition Anggalong on the matter.

As we left Pidyong's house the next morning to go to Anggalong's, Pidyong called after us, "If Anggalong asks you if we are believing, just say we will believe if he believes."

There were several families staying at Anggalong's house when we got there. After the first bit of friendly chitchat, there was a lull in the conversation, and in that lull they all encircled us as if they were waiting for some teaching. It was a pleasant shock to us and, regaining our composure, we got out some Bible pictures and taught them the story of the deliverance of the children of Israel out of Egypt, trusting that through the account of the plagues and the slaying of the first-born, they would understand something of the power of our God.

There was an unmistakable hush in that smoke-stained house as we taught. Everybody listened intently to the lesson. Anggalong's brother, the one who had met us at the stream on our first visit, broke into a profuse sweat. The lesson was so strikingly relevant about Pharaoh hindering God's purposes and then being judged that we turned to Anggalong, asking him if he could afford to stand in God's way by forbidding the Tadyawan Christians to teach in his area.

Anggalong giggled nervously and then replied, "I didn't forbid them to teach; I was only passing on the word from the powerful men in the interior. They are the ones who said it. But they didn't say the Christians couldn't teach anybody; they only said they shouldn't force people into believing in Jesus. They can teach anybody who is interested." Dode and I took a deep breath.

Anggalong was still talking to us, astonishing us by adding, "We'd believe too if it weren't for our fear of those interior men. They're too powerful, and we don't like their curses." He looked afraid.

"If you feel that way," we quickly responded, "then maybe at least you'll let us come in here for longer visits to teach Pidyong and his group because they want the teaching. We'd teach you too if you wanted it."

Anggalong hedged. "Maybe I'd better go into the interior first and ask those tough ones in there."

Anggalong's brother looked at him and added, "I'll go along with you and we'll warn them what Our Father did to those other men who hindered His work."

Several weeks later, on returning to Pidyong's, though

no one told us, we could guess that the interior men had denied Anggalong any hope of our teaching. Yet, in spite of it, the reactions of Pidyong's people to the gospel perplexed us and kept us perplexed for many visits. At times they seemed on the point of believing in Christ; on other occasions they asked us not to come back any more. Just when we ourselves were beginning to doubt any real victory for Christ in that place, they surprised us by building a doll's house of a hut for us. They said it was ours to live in when we came in to teach them. It was an encouraging sign, and we were elated with joy. But then, just as suddenly, on the next visit Pidyong's attitude had taken a right-about-face. He began to mock openly and was rude. One morning, sitting there on our floor with the others listening to our teaching on prayer, he, with sarcastic slurs, cut in and sneered, "Our Father doesn't give me what I ask for. He doesn't give me my money. I do the work and the Filipinos give me my money. I go to the forest. I jump on the rattan to make it snap down. I carry it home. I split it. I remove its inner pulp and scrape it clean. And I carry it down to the Filipinos. They are the ones who give me the money for it." Smugly he leaned back against a pole of the house, satisfied with himself and his contradiction.

The Lord had an answer for Pidyong. "But who gives you the health and strength to do all that?" we asked. "Our Father could let you get sick and weak so that you wouldn't be able to work. Then what?"

Pidyong's wife and two other women nodded their heads with wide open eyes, and then turned on him, relief in their voices, "They're right. Oh, we understand that. It *is* Our Father."

On our very next visit coldness and fear pervaded the air. The folk talked to us only when we asked them a direct question. Even the three women stayed away from us. The first few hours dragged agonizingly slowly. Finally Pidyong came over to our hut and, squatting on the ground at the bottom of the pole that led up to our doorway, frankly told us what he had in mind. "I'm just like a man who has a load to carry on his back," he explained. "When I look at the load, I'm not sure whether or not I want to carry it. So I pick it up and try it out. If I don't like it, I put it down again. And that's what I've done with your teaching. I've tried it out and I don't want it any more."

"But if you all would trust Christ, you wouldn't have to fear these other men and the demons," we urged.

"I'm not afraid of them," he boasted. "I just don't want your teaching." It was hard to take. Here was the man who just one-and-a-half years previously had said, "It doesn't matter if my wife believes, or my leader believes, or my people believe. This is what I want." And now he was rejecting the Lord with undisputed finality.

The three women were not so dogmatic. "We can't believe if Pidyong doesn't believe," they excused themselves. "We'll go on praying and believing in our hearts, though, and the others won't know anything about it. But we don't want you here any more."

Pidyong concluded the matter a few moments later, erasing any hope that this was only a temporary set-back as on other previous visits; "If ever we change our minds and want your teaching again, we know where you live in town and we'll come to get you." It was too conclusive for us to miss the point. We knew their fear of the death curse compelled them to make this choice. It was Katubo's all over again—another seeming victory for the demons. We packed our few belongings and made the weary climb up the mountain, then down the trail back to town, praying only one prayer, "Lord, in your fullness of time, open up this work again. Why should the devil have the last word in this place?"

23 Frustrations

Dode and I were outside weeding one morning, weeding being on our weekly schedule since snakes didn't like cleared land and we didn't like snakes. "Where are you going?" we called to some of the men who passed by the church grounds.

"We're just looking around," they replied, nodding their heads in different directions. "We're trying to figure out where it would be best to plant our rice this year. It's getting harder and harder to decide because more and more of the Filipinos are moving in, taking whatever land they want. Just the other day a Filipino came in and burnt off some land where what's-his-name's fruit trees were growing. All the trees died, including the few coffee trees he had. It's a real shame."

"Yes, I guess I was lucky," said Panot, weakly smiling, "at least the man who came into *my* territory didn't burn down my coconut trees.'

"You mean he claimed some of your land?" we inquired.

"Yes," Panot replied, "he came to see me, carrying some of my coconut seedlings which he had uprooted. He said he was ready to burn off the land and he felt it would be a pity to burn them down along with everything else. He told me to plant them somewhere else because he wanted the land they were growing on. In fact, he said he already owned the land." Panot searched our faces. "How could he get it if I have applied for the title deeds?"

For Dode and me this land problem was the most frustrating and sickening of all in the everyday life of the tribesman. It was not confined only to the Tadyawan tribe. Land-snatching was happening all over the island of Mindoro, and the tribesmen were at the mercy of the snatchers. Filipinos invaded the mountains, carrying false pieces of paper, shoving them under the noses of illiterate tribesmen and telling them it was their deed to the land the tribesmen were living on and that they'd have to leave. Others came in and offered the tribesman a small sum of money for his long-cultivated land; and the tribesman, ignorant of the value of money and thinking he was rich, would accept the pittance and move off the land, unknowingly forfeiting his privilege of squatter's rights to the only land he could legally claim.

It was a happy day for us all when the Philippine Government, awaking to the needs of the existing tribes in their country, appointed a Commission on National Integration, whose responsibility was the preservation and gradual integration of the minority groups. They sent a representative to Mindoro Island, a man who himself was a tribesman from another island, but now educated and employed by the Government. Friendly and eager to help them, he was well liked by the Mindoro tribesmen. He had hoped to get land reservations for them but, when that plan fell through, he encouraged them to make application for their land, claiming squatter's rights. Many from all the tribes lodged papers with the Bureau of Forestry but, disappointingly enough, the Bureau was not in as big a hurry to process the tribesmen's papers as they were the Filipinos' papers. It was a long, heart-breaking delay.

"The Bureau must have lots of work to do. Maybe your papers are all at the bottom of a huge pile," we tried to comfort. "A lot of tribespeople have applied for land, the Iraya, Alangan, Hanunoo, Buhid—in fact, I understand that the Buhid have all paid their fifteen-peso fees already; so they're one step ahead. Maybe you'll be next."

"How did the Buhid go about paying?" Panot wanted to know, looking as if he'd run straight off to the Bureau to pay his too if it would help matters.

"They went through your representative on the National Integration Commission. He helped them with their papers and collected the money from them, carrying it to the Bureau and filing their papers himself."

"That's great. Hope they soon tell us we can officially file ours. Life here gets pretty hard sometimes. Not only do they take our land away from us, but they steal our other possessions too. The Tawbuid across the river told me that two Sundays ago while they were all at church, they saw some Filipinos go through their village, heading farther west. After church, when the Tawbuid returned to their homes, they found that their houses had been stripped of jungle knives, axes, and food. It's really a wicked thing to do."

"Some men *are* wicked," added Manindok. "That Wakin that we told you about is causing us trouble again too. He's built a big house now right on some of our land, and being so close he threatens us if we won't work for him. He'd never pay us, we know that. And besides, he's evil in other ways, so we don't want to have anything to do with him. Some of our women were bathing down at the river the other day, and Wakin came along half

naked. Our women were frightened and started to run
down the river over the rocks. He chased them, but
fortunately, as they can run better on the rocks than he
can, they got away. I wish he'd leave the area. He's a
wicked man."

"We'll just have to go on trusting Our Father for all
these things," we exhorted, but more to ourselves than to
them, for though we were successful at hiding our own
despair, the despair existed none the less. "Remember,
Our Father says He delights to help defenceless creatures
like widows and orphans; so surely we qualify for His
help right now."

"Yes," they sighed. "Well, we'll go now and see what
we can find," and with that the men walked off single file
down the trail. Only Pedro remained behind the others.
He dug into the little pouch dangling from his neck string
and got out a rag in which he had tied some coins. "I
want another tube of that eye medicine for my wife," he
said. "Her eyes are getting all red and watery again, and
she says they itch persistently." When he got the dirty rag
untied, he quickly sucked in his breath and said, "Oh,
I've got only two *centavos*. Can I bring the other *cinko*
tomorrow?"

"Of course," Dode said, giving him the tube she had
fetched from our room. "And tell your wife to start
putting it in her eyes right away." He tucked the tube into
his pouch and started to go. "Will you be coming to
reading and writing classes tomorrow?" we called. "Your
reading is improving; so you shouldn't miss if you can
help it."

"I'll be coming, but my wife won't come, and she says
she won't be coming to Bible study either. She's been
listening to her father, Bilbino, again," he added,
discouraged. "Bilbino tells her not to bother getting the

good teaching from Our Father. He says he'll give her the good teaching that he gets from his wise-one. She always does whatever Bilbino tells her to do."

"And what about her brother, Bisi—is he listening to Bilbino too? We notice that he hasn't been coming to daily Bible studies lately, though he lives only a few yards away. What do you think is wrong?"

"Bisi doesn't listen to his dad; I know that. He really follows Our Father's words. I don't know why he stopped coming to the Bible studies." He was thoughtful for a moment, sucking air through his teeth. "Maybe he's just lazy," he concluded, and then opened the conversation again: "By the way, do you think Mabilis is getting lazy too? Not about coming to Bible study, but about teaching old Lindogayan. I heard Mabilis tell his wife that it seems useless to teach Lindogayan because he won't listen and just keeps changing the subject."

"Is that what it is!" we interjected. "We knew something had been bothering Mabilis but couldn't figure out what it was. We'll have a talk with him. If that's the case though, he's probably not lazy, just discouraged."

"Oh, yes, maybe. I'll catch up with the others now." And with that Pedro headed down the trail, his new white G-string a bold contrast on his brown body.

Dode and I finished up the weeding for the day, grabbed our laundry pails, some shampoo and clean clothes; and with dust caked under our finger nails and between our toes and clinging to our sweaty bodies, we followed the trail down the steep descent to the river for a good bath.

After lunch that day, Dode, hastened by threatening storm clouds, left the "parsonage" to make a few medical calls, including one to Lindogayan to give him his penicillin injection. While she was gone, I decided to go over to see Mabilis and Atla to find out more about Lindogayan's attitude toward the gospel teaching.

Lindogayan had been in our village only six months. Dode was away on vacation when he and his family first arrived, and Jean Govan, a jolly Irish lass who later joined us permanently, was with me at the time. We were inside the parsonage studying when we first heard unfamiliar voices coming from the top of the hill behind the church. We knew we were getting company, and from the high-pitched tones we knew it would be Tawbuid tribesmen. Apart from us and the small children who were baby-sitting smaller children, our village was deserted, shimmering beneath the ultra heat of midday. Jean and I, not wanting to frighten away our timid forest strangers, secretly peered at them through our window. And what a dark sight we saw as we watched them carefully picking their way down the slanted log that led a hundred feet below to the clearing around the church building and parsonage! There were six of them in all—including a young man carrying a heavy load in a cloth slung from his head and hanging down his back. That load turned out to be his father, Lindogayan. Behind were two women, one carrying an infant; and behind them, a young boy. All of them were dirty, but Lindogayan was by far the dirtiest man Jean and I had ever seen. He hung like a limp lump in the sling on his son's back.

Once down at the bottom of the log, the son stealthily walked across to the middle of the clearing and bent carefully down to unload his human cargo, while the rest of the family rushed to his assistance, putting the old man's feet in the right positions so that he could sit on the ground without falling over. We quietly watched it all, and then when we felt sufficient time had elapsed for them to get used to their surroundings, we slowly walked out through the church toward them. Lindogayan was an ugly sight, miserably filthy, with the accompanying odour intensified by huge tropical ulcers draining with infection. The raw, open ulcer on one leg had eaten right through the bone above his ankle, leaving his foot to dangle uselessly. The ulcer on the other leg extended from ankle to knee; and the large ulcers on the backs of his hands and wrists gnarled and expanded them like stiff fans. The stench was putrid.

Lindogayan, obviously frightened, made no attempt to be friendly. He met our cheerful, welcoming smiles with a scornful look. Not mincing any words or wasting any cordiality, he proclaimed, "We don't believe what you teach. We follow the demons." He wanted medicine for his sores, and that's all he wanted, adding with a haughty tone, "And I won't be paying for it if I don't get well." As far as he was concerned, we weren't going to be friends.

We started the long series of injections willingly but not too hopefully. Dressing his putrefying sores was a challenge to the strongest of stomachs, but we managed, hoping that some day Lindogayan's heart would soften to the gospel. At first he was scornfully adamant against any witness, but gradually as the Tadyawan Christians made a point of dropping in to see him in his little hovel, his heart melted and he responded more amiably. The injections began working miracles; his ulcers got smaller and smaller. He could soon sit up or lie down without anyone aiding him and he even developed the habit of bathing. Before many months passed, he made the statement that he and his family would stay in our village as permanent residents. Who could blame him? Why should he go back to grim heathen darkness amid curses and meannesses and fears when he could live amid happiness and kindness all the time. He granted permission to the rest of his family to attend the church services and agreed to Mabilis and Manindok's coming to teach him every day since he couldn't walk over to the church himself. They had been teaching him for several months until this new opposition came to the fore. I had to find out more about it.

Pleasant chatter from Mabilis's house assured me that he and his family were home.

Coughing to announce my arrival, I made my way up the pole steps and found Mabilis at that moment smiling down on his little girl newly learning to walk. His wife, Atla, sat near her on the floor, laughing and teasing and egging her on. I watched for a while, entering into the fun of it all and then without taking my eyes off his enterprising daughter, addressed Mabilis. "What about Lindogayan, Mabilis? How have you and Manindok been getting along with your teaching of him?" I tried to sound casual and matter-of-fact.

In a flash Mabilis's usual vivacity was gone. His face was crestfallen. "He doesn't believe anything we say," he explained. "Sometimes he won't even listen, but says that he thinks the teaching of the great-grandfathers is better, and he wants to follow that. He keeps interrupting our teaching to tell us what the demons taught him. And not only that, I often see Bilbino dropping by Lindogayan's house, and I've heard them teaching each other demon chants. Last week one of our men overheard Bilbino telling Lindogayan that he should never leave the practices of the demons or spirits of the ancestors. It's pretty hard teaching him under those circumstances. Bilbino's word always carries weight."

"Maybe it would be wise to stop for a while," I

suggested. "But let's pray about it and see." Mabilis nodded, then quickly rushed to rescue his daughter from a crash landing on the bamboo floor. He rubbed her crown, then bounced her into the air while she screamed her pretty little head off. Atla and I smiled at each other.

After daddy got his little girl quieted down to the sniffling stage, Atla asked, "What does the Tagalog word '*saliksik*' mean in our language? I've been reading a Tagalog story, and it had that word in it. I didn't understand the word."

"It's a hard one, all right, but it means to delve into, to investigate," I explained while she rummaged in the wall for her reading materials. Finding the booklet she wanted, she flipped its pages until she found the sentence with the puzzling word in it. Finding it, she read the sentence aloud to see if it really did make sense. Satisfied, she looked up and smiled. She and Mabilis had done well with their Tagalog lessons, as had so many of the other Tadyawan during the long months of daily classes.

"We've got some good news for all of you," I said. "We've invited a Filipino girl to come here for two weeks to hold school in the Tagalog language. She'll help you all she can while she's here. You'll like her. She's a fine Christian. We're hoping to have these schools periodically so that soon some of you will be ready to go off to Bible school for training."

"Who of us will go?" asked Atla.

"It'll be up to the church to decide, because the church will have to look after the fields of those who go to school for the three-month sessions. It's going to mean two three-month periods each year for four years. We'll have to pray about it and ask Our Father to show us who should be sent."

"Yes," joined in Mabilis. "We've got lots of work to do

as it is, but if we all help, we could take care of the students' fields while they're gone; but everybody's got to pitch in, or it won't work."

"Maybe you church elders should bring it up at a meeting some time, so that we can all start thinking about it," I suggested, at the same time looking in the direction of the tiny window. "Hey, look at those clouds," I exclaimed. "They're right on top of us. I'd better be going lest I get drenched. Mabilis, I think this is Pedro's Sunday to lead the Communion service, isn't it? Be sure to remind him to get the sugar cane juice ready and the sweet potato roasted."

I hardly heard his "yes" as I dashed out of the house to beat the imminent cloudburst. On the trail back to our house I met Manindok's wife hurriedly carrying Samuel back to their home. "Say," I paused to remark, "he's getting fatter. And look, he's trying to smile."

"Yes," she assured me with a wide grin, "but he's still all paralysed down the right side. That's why his face looks so funny. Only one side moves. He's feeling better, though, we can tell." I agreed with her. To have Samuel smile was really an accomplishment after almost two years of continual irritability until he lapsed into lifelessness. A streak of lightning and a thundering crash sent us both skeltering in opposite directions for our homes. I heard big drops fall on the leaves, first one here, then one there. I raced, clambered up the pole steps and thudded into the church. Dode was already at the fireplace putting on the tea kettle. Breathless, I sank down on the floor beside her while she blew up the fire. Then down it came—huge drops pelting thunderously on the thatched roof.

"I just saw Samuel with his mother," I shouted

between breaths. "He's gaining weight and looks hopeful of recovery. He actually tried to smile."

"That's great," Dode shouted back. "We'll soon have to get him on some kind of therapy to see if he can learn to walk again and get those muscles moving."

"Any ideas?"

"Some low fences, maybe, so that he can hold on to something at first. But it'll be like pulling teeth to get him started because those stiff little legs will really ache."

"Speaking of teeth," I interjected without really meaning to change the subject, "Pedro has finally agreed to go to the dentist in town to have that old molar stump pulled out. Won't that be a milestone in Tadyawan records! He's scared about it all, but he says he'll go. Hope he keeps his word; then maybe others bothered by rotten teeth will overcome their fears and go too."

"I surely hope so. I'd hate to have to learn dentistry when I'm home on furlough!" Dode joked, as she poured tea into our mugs.

"How'd you get on with Lindogayan? Was he friendly?" I asked.

"Yes, he was glad for another injection now that he sees how well his ulcers are healing, but he was unresponsive to anything I tried to say about the Lord. No wonder Mabilis and Manindok are discouraged."

"It'll be interesting to see how it all turns out," I mused aloud while sipping the first sip of good, hot tea. "We don't seem to be taking any territory from the enemy lately, not in Lindogayan's life anyway. And I'm worried about Bisi, Dode; surely it's more than laziness that keeps him away from the Bible studies. He always used to come faithfully morning and night. I wonder what it is . . . ?"

24 Maturing

Several months passed. Bisi remained in the shadows, spasmodically attending the Bible studies and church services but not showing much interest even when he did attend. It worried us. But if he was slipping backward, several more were coming into understanding. Fourteen of them asked for baptism. We put it to the church of twelve, asking them if they wanted to examine the fourteen that had submitted their names for baptism. "Oh no, not all of them," they answered us immediately. "There's no sense in examining Bayengbeng, for she hasn't left the old life. We still hear her chanting to the demons. And Sabil isn't yet ready for baptism either. She insisted that her husband Kalobang chant to one of the demons when their son was ill not so very long ago; so there's no point in examining her, or Kalobang either for that matter, because he shouldn't have listened to her. We'll do the rest, though."

Examination afternoon seemed interminably long. The examiners sat on the church floor in a circle, and one by one the candidates were called into the church and made to sit in the middle of the circle. For the timid ones it was sheer agony to have to sit under the scrutiny of twelve pairs of eyes, while twelve mouths shot questions at them, and twelve pairs of attentive ears sorted answers in search of proof that they were truly born again and eligible for baptism. Some took it more bravely than others. Dolilaw approached the church steps and entrance, giggling all the way, with head completely shrouded in her dirty brown blanket. She peered out of the bottom of it to get her footing. Her answers to the questions were barely audible, but the church knew she had been walking with the Lord for some time, and they passed her.

Next was her husband, Marcos, the man of few words. For as long as we knew him, he chose to be the quiet man in the background, working hard with the others when he agreed with them, working hard alone when he didn't. He was a man of the forest, strong and capable, a man who felled magnificent trees, carried tremendous loads, and endured all kinds of forest hardship and sorrow; but during his examination he shrivelled up with terror before his own friends and relatives on the examining committee. Yet, though questions flew at him fast, he answered well. Yes, he wanted to be baptized because Our Jesus had taken away his sin, and he wanted folk to know it. Yes, he would come to the church services as long as he was able to. Yes, if he were sick and couldn't come, he would pray and study at home. Yes, he was available for evangelistic trips. The usual questions over, Marcos relaxed slightly, but then Panot turned his head in Marcos's direction, raised his eyebrows, and shot him a pointed question that nobody had ever been asked before: "Marcos, you've been making a lot of promises here. Who have you been making these promises to? To us or to Our Father?" It was obvious that Marcos was taken aback. His nostrils enlarged, his eyes darted all around the room, landing on the ceiling. With voice uncontrollably inaudible, he struggled to get his answer out, "These are my promises to Our Father."

"Good," said Panot with feeling. "That's really the best, because we are only men like you, and you might find it easy to break your promises to us; but if you have made the promises to Our Father, you will keep them." Panot beamed with pleasure, and we knew that no matter what else happened during Marcos' interview, Panot had already accepted him for baptism.

The youngest one to ask for baptism was Dorcas, another shy miss, cute and lively, industrious in her work and keen to remember all the Bible lessons. At that very time Dorcas was of marriageable age, and her heathen parents were negotiating for a heathen husband, the whole affair causing the church much apprehension concerning her baptism. They put her through some of the routine questions and then, wanting to be sure they'd make no mistake in their decision, asked, "Dorcas, you know there is no Christian man in this community that can marry you, and there are no other Christians yet in other areas that would be eligible. What will you do if Our Father doesn't give you a Christian husband? Will you hunt for a husband among the heathen?" The terrified little lady mumbled her answer from under her hood. It was a "no". One of the examiners sitting near Dorcas relayed her answer to the rest, but they were not satisfied. "Dorcas, you'll have to say it loud so that we all can hear. We want to hear it from your own mouth that you will not take a heathen husband, so that we'll be sure." The little frightened bird managed to get the answer out so that all could hear and be satisfied. We pitied her, knowing how painful this experience was to her, but months afterward we were grateful that the church had been so insistent.

Her parents, wanting to be free from their responsibility to find her a husband, put much pressure on her in the early months following her baptism, trying to force her into agreeing to marry the heathen young man who had asked for her. He had already had three successive wives and was himself a drunkard; but he was a sparkling suitor, and to the church it became apparent that Dorcas was succumbing to his attention. Little woman heart. She wanted a husband—what tribal girl didn't?—and he seemed the only available young man in the area at the time. From all we heard, Dorcas was beginning to weaken. "Oh," the village insisted, "she likes him, we know, because she gets noisy and giggly when he's around, trying to attract his attention. We're afraid that with her parents' insistence one of these days she'll just run off with him. He's desperate to have her, comes around often and says he'll never stop pestering until she is married to him."

"Is it time, then, for the church and Dorcase to talk things over?" we asked.

"Yes," they said. "We'd better do it before it's too late. She's beginning to like him more and more."

It was a solemn occasion when the whole church got together; even those not yet baptized sat in on that session. They plied Dorcas with questions, trying to discern how she really felt. Bisi, though himself straying, as far as we could tell, appeared to be quite upset over this potential disobedience to Our Father. He took the lead in the whole affair. But we were getting nowhere with Dorcas. Either shyness or shame or both kept her from answering anything, not even with a shake of the head. She just sat there through question after question about whether or not she really liked the man. And then came the question, "Dorcas, you were asked about this when you were baptized, and you promised at that time that you would not marry a heathen man. Are you going to go back on your promise to Our Father?" Dorcas reddened, quickly hid her face behind her cape, and sat there in crumpled silence. We all silently and prayerfully waited through dragging minutes. Finally Bisi broke the silence, "Well, that's it," he said, getting up and going over to join Mabilis at the fireplace. Then turning to Dode and me, he explained, "In our culture when people don't answer 'no' to a question like that, it means that their answer is 'yes'. Dorcas intends to break her promise to Our Father." The others nodded in agreement. But then one further suggestion saved the day, "Dorcas, if you are too frightened to speak, will you write your answer on a piece of paper?" And with that Dorcas stood up and made one dash out of the church door and up the trail to her home. Several of the smaller children chose to run after her.

We were a mournful group around the fireplace. "You see," said Bisi turning to us, "the group has asked me to go to see the young man and tell him to stop pursuing Dorcas, but how can I when she might really want him? If I could go and tell him to stop it because she doesn't want him, that would be right. I'd go under those conditions." Sitting around the fireplace for some time, hardly talking, we waited for Dorcas's note—if she was going to write one—and trusted for a spiritual victory that day. Finally one of the little children stood in the doorway with outstretched hand, a small piece of paper held between his fingers. Reluctant, but eager, we all read the note. "I will not forsake my promise to Our Father. What I promised Him before I mean to follow even now." What a relief to the whole church! The matter was settled. Now they were strengthened to stand firm in their denial of the young man, and he eventually stopped his pursuit. Dorcas was spared, but only temporarily, for another temptation came her way through Lindogayan, who aspired to great things for his youngest son.

One Sunday morning after the church service the Tadyawan announced to us that Lindogayan said they should all help to build him a new house. He wanted a big house like theirs.

"Yes," someone else added, "he says that if we're really Christians like we say we are and the Lord has changed our lives, we should be kind to him and his family and build them a nice house."

"That's right." Manindok was enthusiastic. "We should all work together; then he'll really stay in our village and believe in Our Jesus."

We didn't like the sound of it. "Is that the way to build Christ's church?" we cautioned. "Just think a minute. He's challenging you to build them a house to prove your Christianity to him. But haven't you proved it already? You've shared your food with them because they had no source of food when they came here. You've been kind to them. Mabilis and Manindok have gone over every day to teach him Our Father's words. Is it right for him to demand more? Remember, some people followed Our Jesus only because they wanted the bread, but they never really believed."

"Shouldn't we really build them a house then?" Manindok asked sincerely, but obviously disappointed, for he was bent on getting folks into the Kingdom no matter what the means. The outcome at Pidyong's was still too fresh a defeat on Manindok's heart.

"Will Lindogayan's wife and son and daughter-in-law help with the building?" we inquired.

"No," came the answer. "He says they have lots of other work to do."

"Well, then, you really shouldn't do it," we said, "but if you really feel that you should, why not tell Lindogayan you will if his son and the two women help too. That would be a happy compromise."

Satisfied with that suggestion, they accepted it and put it to Lindogayan. Before very long a nice house was ready for Lindogayan and his family. It didn't deepen his interest in the Word of God, however, and shortly he was dissatisfied again. He demanded that they prove their Christianity by helping his son to make a big field for their rice crop so that they'd have plenty to eat after harvest. Making fields was always a community effort, so this would have been in keeping with things. But everybody helped everybody else; Lindogayan's son never helped anybody and didn't intend to.

Manindok got quite upset over this episode. "But we've got to help," he pleaded. "He says that if we don't make a field for him, he'll leave the village." The expression on Manindok's face looked as if he already felt guilty of the blood of Lindogayan.

Like a bomb our next words shattered their misguided hopes. "He can leave if he really wants to," we said undisturbed. The people—and Manindok especially—looked horrified, as if by our words we were condemning the whole family to a Christless eternity. "You see," we patiently instructed, "his blood wouldn't be on our hands. We've all given him the Word of Our Father, and Our Father is pleased with that. He doesn't hold us responsible if he won't believe. We've done what we could; that is all Our Father asks. If they leave, it'll be because they reject Our Father's Word, which is what they've been doing right along. You yourselves have told us that they steal your possessions from your houses and the vegetables from your gardens, and Mabilis says that Lindogayan mocks at the teaching from Our Father's Word."

The Tadyawan church understood what we were trying to tell them, and in understanding were relieved. But for some reason Lindogayan stayed and eventually the Tadyawan helped his son with a new field. Having gained another victory, Lindogayan didn't stop there. One day he said to the men, "You have two nice young girls here.

Give me one of them for a wife for my younger son. And if you don't give me one of them, we'll all leave your village." One of the girls he wanted was Dorcas, who was still single, still hopeful. But the church was instantly firm on this occasion. They would not give either of the girls to Lindogayan's son, with Dorcas herself confirming her disinterest. She didn't want this unbeliever. Lindogayan and his family made plans to leave and early one morning quietly slipped out of the village, going back to utter darkness and demon domination.

25 Hope for Kardo

Dode and I packed up our last-minute belongings and closed up the house in town, grateful that we had made our deadline and were ready to return to the Tadyawan hills with all of our lesson materials mimeographed and stapled for use. Usually we were eager to get back to the Tadyawan, but this time we were heavy hearted because we had some mournful news for them concerning their land.

"How shall we tell them?" Dode asked, making a final check to see that each window was tightly shut against tropical storms.

I sighed. I knew what she meant. For several years we had been exhorting the Tadyawan to trust the outside world, and it wasn't easy. How could they trust when the outside world had done nothing to inspire trust but, on the contrary, had taken every possible advantage of the timid tribesman, cheating him, tricking him, and making unreasonable demands upon him and his time? Initially, we had been happy to co-operate with the government's programme of integration, but how could we go on wholeheartedly encouraging it when it meant nothing but heartache upon heartache for the tribesman? This latest news was by far the most disturbing. I packed our sandwiches in the top of my army pack and zipped it up. "We'll just have to tell them exactly how things stand and trust the Lord to keep them from becoming harder of heart in the situation," I replied unenthusiastically. We both sighed.

Several months back the Tadyawan, responding to our strong urgings, had sought and followed the advice of the Filipino representative on the National Integration Commission concerning making application as homesteaders on their land. We had just recently learned, while in town, that that man had turned out to be dishonest. Perhaps handling other people's money proved too big a temptation for him; for he had cheated the government out of funds, and the money he had collected from tribesmen on the island for their land applications had never been paid into the Bureau of Forestry but was instead pocketed for his own personal use. For a tribesman to save fifteen *pesos* [about £2] meant a lot of hard work and denying himself the occasional luxury of a can of sardines purchased at the town market. And then to have it all come to nothing! It was more than disheartening—it was sickening. We wearily locked the front door and left the house for the Tadyawan hills.

Quite a delegation of Tadyawan had come out to the road to carry in our month's supply of food. As we walked along the trail, weighed down with our heavy loads and weary from the long hike in the tropical sun, we broke the news to them, praying that they would not doubt us or Our Father, who had for some reason allowed this another trial to come into their lives. The Lord answered our prayer; they showed disappointment and frustration, but no bitterness. They were now back where they started as far as their land was concerned, and they had no one to turn to for help.

But a man's life is more precious to him than his land, and soon the Tadyawans' land problem was engulfed by a more terrifying problem. We had been in the hills about a month when Pedro breathlessly bounced into the church and, without even waiting for us to appear in the doorway of the parsonage, shouted out to us, "Remember Wakin, that we told you about—that wicked Filipino who lives near some of our church families?" And hardly pausing to hear our answer he hastened on to say, "The Tawbuid across the river have just told us that he shot one of their leaders, Gorang by name." We knew Gorang; he was a big brawny tribesman.

"Why did he shoot him?" we asked dismayed.

"He went into Gorang's house and demanded that he get off the land, but when Gorang said he wouldn't, Wakin got out his gun and in anger shot Gorang twice through the neck right in front of his wife and little children. Then Wakin left. Gorang's wife was so frightened when she saw her husband dead that she ran away with her children. She's with relatives back in the interior and says she'll never come back to her house again. The news has spread all around. The police in town learned about it too because that kind Filipino who always helps us reported it to them. Now they say that Wakin has run away; at least nobody can find him. He hasn't been seen since it happened, but we're afraid he'll be back again because his wife is still living there in their house."

"Did the police do anything about it?" we asked.

"They hiked all the way into these hills to see," Pedro said, "and then do you know what they did? They cut off Gorang's head to take to town as evidence that he had been shot. Evidently nobody in town wanted to believe the story—thought it was all lies that we had invented."

We were horrified. "What are they going to do about it?"

"They say they can't do anything about it because they don't have anyone to swear an affidavit. Gorang's wife was the only witness, and she will never come out of the interior. She's afraid Wakin will come back and shoot her next. She says he can have the land."

"So Wakin is left to his own devices!"

"Yes," affirmed Pedro, fearfully. "He may be hiding right here somewhere in these mountains. He'll wait until it all blows over. We're all frightened. Remember a couple of years ago when he said he'd kill me and my brother-in-law? Somebody told us that years ago Wakin had murdered a man in one of the towns and had come here to our mountains to hide from the authorities. He's really a wicked one."

The news kept us and all the Tadyawan stirred up for several weeks. Dode actually ran into Wakin in the company of others one day along the trail—a murderer, free as a bird because there was no eyewitness to testify against him. Then later we heard that he had gone to another town and there died of a heart attack. While the Tadyawan believed this story, I could only wonder if it were really so or if he had left by boat to another island, only to live the same kind of life again. It was an awesome thought.

But Wakin was gone and that was what mattered to the Tadyawan. The relief from that fear was welcome. Panot was especially grateful and expressed his gratitude at the prayer meeting one Sunday.

It was the Sunday Pedro led the meeting. Pedro was never shy otherwise, but when he had to lead one of the meetings, it took all the courage he could summon to do it. That Sunday he sat in the leader's spot on the floor in front of the chattering, gossiping group, with his head bent over his hymnbook, leafing aimlessly through its pages as he waited for everybody to arrive; we never started a meeting until all were present or accounted for. The stragglers were arriving one by one, some in their pitiful rags, some still dripping from the bath they had taken in the river along the way, and others, with a flair for apeing the outside world, dressed in their town-bought clothes, ill-fitted or uncomfortably hanging down to their ankles. As the attendance swelled, the more deafening the chatter became. The church was full, but still Pedro waited. We all knew who he was waiting for. It was old Boganyan, whose home was only ten yards from the church but who, for some reason, seemed to like being the last one to arrive at the services. When some of the heads in the doorway turned toward the outside steps, we knew Boganyan was making his appearance. The Tadyawan seated in the doorway were tightly squeezed together and couldn't, or teasingly wouldn't, make a path for him to enter. Not to be deterred, Boganyan stretched from the steps, shinnied along the outside poles of the church and pulled away some palm branches of the wall. As he climbed through the hole he had made, grinning triumphantly at all of us, Lutero suddenly shouted, "Hey, look. Thief! Thief! A thief has just entered our church." Everybody screeched with delight, everybody, that is, except Dode and me. We looked with consternation. Laughingly they explained to us, "We've just recently been studying about the shepherd and his sheep from Our Father's Word, and He says that the one who doesn't enter through the door but comes in some other way is a thief." And they all laughed again, shouting and pointing to Boganyan, "Thief! Thief!" Boganyan continued to grin.

Now that Boganyan had arrived, Pedro, regardless of the good humoured commotion, with head still bent, weakly announced that our meeting would begin. Only those very close to him on the floor heard his announcement, but they speedily buzzed the word around and soon heads were bowing for what was left of Pedro's prayer, for he had plunged right into praying, waiting for nothing. Prayer over, he rushed into mumbling the number of our first hymn and, unlike Mabilis who preached a sermonette on every hymn he chose, Pedro quickly started singing though no one had yet found the page. It was agony to Dode and me. It was no problem to the Tadyawan, however, and they sang lustily once they found the page. But if the opening exercises were rushed, the prayer time was not, and one by one the Tadyawan prayed for themselves, for the unsaved members of their families, for Pidyong and his leader Anggalong as well as for the others there at Pasi. Then they branched out in prayer for other areas. "We only ask You," one concluded his prayer, "to help us to teach these people so that they won't spend all of the future in the big fire." "Amen" grunts came from all corners of the room. Their concern for others was deepening.

When prayer time was over, as no one seemed in a hurry to leave, Pedro called for testimonies. "I thank Our Father for healing my little girl's broken leg," said Marcos. "We were really frightened that day she fell out of our house down on to the ground below. We thought she'd never walk again. But she is walking and running and playing."

Manindok was one big smile. "I praise Our Father for His goodness to us. Samuel is much better, and he is learning to walk again." Everybody agreed with great joy. Samuel had become one happy, persevering little fellow. With the whole community's co-operation and encouragement he had learned to hold on to the little fences that Dode had engineered, and he was managing to walk for longer and longer stretches. We all knew he was on the way. His little muscles would become stronger.

Lutero wanted to give a testimony too. "I thank Our Father for keeping us safe the other day when we hitched a ride on a lumber truck. We were headed for town. The truck had lots of heavy logs on it and when we came to a steep incline, two of the wheels got into a rut and we thought we'd overturn. Some of us managed to jump off the other side. It never did overturn, though."

Then there was a pause. "Anybody else?" asked Pedro. Panot was looking up at the roof mentally struggling over something, obviously wanting to give some kind of a testimony. Pedro noticed him and said, "You, Panot, do you want to say anything?" Panot bent over, spat through the floor, then scratched his thigh characteristically. It seemed he could never speak in public without first spitting and then scratching, but usually, once that was over, he spoke with freedom. On this occasion, however, he hedged a bit longer, wrinkled up his whole face and hunched his shoulders. A smile appeared across his lips, but was quickly hidden behind his stubby hand. Putting his hand down again, he said, "This isn't going to be very nice to say, but it *is* an answer to prayer." There was another long pause. "I was always afraid of that Wakin because he was so evil, even to our women. I prayed that Our Father would remove him from our area so that we could live in peace, and now Our Father has removed him. The reason he's gone isn't very nice to think about, but he *is* gone." Panot threw his head back and stared at the roof waiting for the reaction of the others to this testimony that sounded so unloving and unchristian. But nobody disapproved. They all understood, for they all felt the same relief.

After a few more testimonies of praise, Dode and I ventured one. "We've got a testimony too, but it began a long time ago. Do you think you have time to listen to it? And do you think you can all stay awake in this heat?" They laughed with us, assuring us that they could and tacitly agreeing that the usual ones would be asleep no matter what.

"Do you remember our telling you about Katubo and his people at Taghikan?" When they nodded, we went on. "Well, after we left their area and before we came to live with you folks, we trekked all over the Tadyawan mountains teaching people that we met along the way, hoping that one day somebody would be interested enough in Our Father's Word to invite us in to live with them and teach them more. In all our travels we found one group that did seem interested. They lived in the interior of the Aglobang River valley and, while they didn't understand very much, they wanted to hear more. They became friendly and were not afraid to ask questions about Our Father. One woman couldn't understand how He would make her clean from all her sin. Said she, 'How will He do it? Will He take me to the river to wash me?'" The Tadyawan nudged each other.

"We didn't understand that either, when you first told

us," they interjected. We smiled. They had come a long way.

"One of them," we continued, "asked us one day if he had to shout really loud when he prayed, so that Our Father would be able to hear him way up there in heaven." Again there were a few titters from the congregation. "They didn't understand how they could pray to Our Father anyway, because, they explained, nobody knew their language but themselves. 'Does Our Father understand our language?' they asked us."

Knowing better now, our Tadyawan laughed again and then commented, "That's exactly what we wondered when you first taught us. When we saw you writing out words on your papers, we thought you were going to teach them to Our Father so that He'd understand us when we prayed to Him. We were really surprised when you told us that He already knew everybody's language."

"And did you wonder about us too, like they did?" we asked. "One of the women on the Aglobang touched our skin and then inquired, 'Is the skin under your clothes white too?'"

Again our Tadyawan laughed, saying, "Us too—that's what we wondered." Everybody was feeling cozy by then and settled down more and more to hear our story.

"After a few happy visits with these Aglobang people, we began to notice that they looked suspicious of us, not quite so friendly, and sometimes afraid. Then secretly they moved away. Only after they moved did we learn that some Filipinos had told them that we were wicked women who would kidnap their children and carry them away to a school in our own land. We never saw the people again."

"What a pity!" they chorused. And then they looked at

us again as if to say that that was a funny testimony to end on such a defeated note.

"But wait, that's not the whole story," we continued. "On one of our previous visits to those Aglobang Tadyawan, we were walking along the rocks beside the river and met a man brave enough to be travelling alone. We were impressed. Everything about him spelled strength—broad shoulders and a muscular body that even his torn red T-shirt over his G-string couldn't conceal. His eyes were alert and taking everything in. We stopped him and tried to talk with him, turning the conversation into some teaching. He liked it, told us his name was Kardo, and——"

"Kardo!" interrupted Kalobang. "I've heard of him. He's a leader of one of the groups in that Aglobang area. He has a big following."

"Yes, that's what he told us," we went on. "He said he wished we would come and teach his people what we had just finished teaching him. We assured him we would and, because he was going away to settle some tribal business and couldn't turn around to take us to his place, we asked him about the trail to his house, promising that we would visit sometime soon. But in spite of his directions, we could never find the trail."

Our congregation waited. Some of the folk were getting drowsy, for it was a terribly hot day. Boganyan, who had slept through much of the earlier service was now sound asleep. Bayengbeng returned to a state of temporary consciousness only when her chin dropped on to her chest. The babies were all asleep in their mothers' laps, while some of the smaller children slept soundly on the church floor. The older children had gone outside to play.

"For some months we wondered if we'd ever find

Kardo's place and decided to make one more attempt. Before leaving our house in town we prayed that Our Father would make it possible for us to find them, and He did. It was a strange thing, but the logging trucks belonging to the sawmill were not going into the interior in those days; so with some Filipinos we hitched a ride on a private truck that came along. When we hopped on, at the back end of the truck, we stood face to face with Kardo, who had also hailed the truck a little earlier, further down the road. From the expression on Kardo's face, we gathered that he was as surprised as we were. 'Where are you two going?' he asked us. We wasted no time. 'We're going to your place if you'll take us,' we answered; and the matter was settled.

"When we alighted from the truck, Kardo took us by the hand and led us through the river. Then, with him taking the lead, we climbed a mountain slope and hiked along narrow trails until we came to a small clearing in the middle of the forest where he and his people lived. Not many of the older folk were at home—maybe they were off to their fields—but Kardo sat talking with us and asking us questions. Every so often he ordered one of the children to go to somebody's house and invite them to come. He explained to us that he wanted all his people to hear Our Father's Word, and then he confidentially added, 'After everybody gets here, I want you two women to look all around to see which of my people have wickedness within them. When you know, tell me and I'll tell them what they can do about it just like you've been telling me.'"

"How strange!" interrupted the Tadyawan. "Why, everybody's got sin in his heart. And besides, nobody can see into the inner being of a man. Only Our Father can do that."

"Yes," I went on, "but don't forget that Kardo was hearing Our Father's words for the first time. There was lots he didn't know, but he did catch on to some things very quickly. Listen to this. In the course of the conversation we talked about the beautiful but daunting expanse of Mindoro's forest and how hard it was for us to trek around in it without getting lost. I told him that I was particularly poor at figuring out directions and that it was a good thing I always had a companion or I would get lost in the forest and would just die there. It confused Kardo. His bright eyes flashed in my direction as he said quietly, 'No, you wouldn't get lost; if you were by yourself, I think your Jesus would help you!'"

Many *hmmmmmm's* were muttered throughout the room. They appreciated Kardo's conclusions after knowing so little. Those who were awake were keen with interest by now.

"Kardo and his people all thought the message was so good that they insisted that we all pray together and ask Our Father to take away their sin so that they would go to heaven when they died. I tried to dissuade them, explaining that maybe they should wait until they understood more clearly, but as they refused to be delayed, we prayed with them. I remember Kardo's prayer: 'My Father, I'm Kardo. Take away all my sin.'"

"Are they all believers, then?" the Tadyawan congregation asked us, amazed that believing would be so fast in any community.

"No," we explained, shifting our position, for our legs were getting numb under us. "They didn't know what it would cost to leave the demon world. They thought they could do it and said they would. But they really couldn't make the break. They continued obeying the commands of the demons while at the same time trying to walk with

Our Father. We learned that from them later. Anyway, they invited us to return, and we promised we would— but the next time we went, the Aglobang River was flooded, and we couldn't get across. We tried a second time. The river was still flooded. Some months later, when the dry season had come, we tried again and found the trail to their houses. But when we got there, nobody was living there any more. All the cooking pots and baskets were gone, and the house was beginning to fall apart. Only the cockroaches remained behind."

Again our Tadyawan looked at each other and laughed, some of them stretching out and lying on the floor, propping their heads against the big poles that went down the centre of the church floor. We were glad that they were still listening.

"We never saw Kardo again, for we couldn't find out where they had moved. And besides, by that time we had met you folks and you had invited us in here to teach you; so we felt Our Father was asking us to come here." They looked pleased. "But," unflagging, we went on, ourselves slouching down further against the wall supporting our tired backs—this had been a long prayer meeting— "listen to this now. The day we first went to the town market to meet Pidyong, we ran into another tribesman all by himself." They raised their eyebrows. "Yes, it was Kardo," we said. "We explained to him all about not being able to find them and assured him that if they would like, we would come and teach them again."

"Did you go right away?" they asked eagerly.

"No, we couldn't because then not only were we coming in here to teach you, but we were also visiting Pidyong's area and teaching them. It didn't seem to be Our Father's time. But now we think it is."

"Will you go then?" they asked, eagerly stirring.

"We'd like to, but we feel it'd be a good idea if some of you evangelists went with us."

Sabil agreed with us and wasted no time in saying so. "Some of you men ought to go," she spoke importantly. "It's too far for our two sisters to carry heavy packs, and it's too lonely for them too. They need you men to protect them." The men agreed. Prayer meeting ended on a very happy note, and already Dode and I were envisaging a Tadyawan church on the Aglobang River. The dream, however, was premature.

26 Another Snare Holds

Kardo and his household welcomed Panot, Kalobang, Dode and me warmly when we panted into their large house one mid-afternoon. Their friendliness and attentiveness to the Word of God was more than we had dared to hope, and when it came time for goodbyes three days later, they showed not the slightest hesitation about wanting us to visit again, and we, likewise without any hesitation, agreed to return soon.

When we did return we were in for even bigger surprises, for Kardo had circulated the news and many of the more brave and curious tribespeople under his rule came to see us and to listen to our teaching. Eager Panot seized every available moment to witness in conversations or to teach whoever wanted to listen or whenever a newcomer arrived at the house. Kardo, showing a real liking for Panot, listened to him for long hours, sitting opposite him at the fireplace plying him with thoughtful question after question. Panot's sincerity and gracious manner allowed him to be inoffensively frank. Noticing that Kardo and all of his children were wearing shiny silver crosses around their necks—crosses that Kardo had purchased at the town market—Panot said, "Friend, your whole family's wearing these crosses, and you think they'll protect you; but not us—we do not trust in the ornament; it's the Man on the cross we trust. When He died, all of the sin of everybody in the whole world was placed on Him. That's why we say He paid for our sin. The price He paid was His body." Kardo nodded comprehendingly, then leaned back against a pole quietly thinking.

Later he edged closer to Panot and said, "Teach me the songs so that I can sing them and go to heaven."

Panot's eyes enlarged greatly, a habit he had whenever he disagreed with anybody. "Friend," he mildly admonished, "it doesn't matter how well or how much you sing the songs. The thing that matters is, have you left your old life?" Kardo was captivated. But not everyone in the house was, for they constantly shot furtive glances at Dode and me or at Kalobang who was also off to one side teaching some of thé younger fellows and girls. Among the apprehensive ones was a tall, thin, unattractive tribesman, with buck-teeth and a red betel-nut mouth. What he lacked in looks, however, was compensated for by his effervescent personality. He took the lead in the conversation of the frightened group near him and often bubbled over with a joke to relieve their strain. While Kalobang was still teaching, this buck-toothed man raised himself on his haunches and scuttled over to where Kalobang was sitting. "Is it all right with you if I feel the calf of your leg?" he asked.

Kalobang was completely taken off guard. His eyelids

fluttered and he looked all about him. Then, shifting to stretch out his legs from under him, he said uncertainly, "Why sure, go ahead."

The buck-toothed man reached out his hand, gingerly at first, but then with added pressure against Kalobang's leg, looking more amazed with each squeeze. In great wonder he turned to all the men in his group and said, "Oh my, it's hard, just like ours!"

Kalobang giggled girlishly in his bewilderment. "Friend," he asked frowning, "why did you do that?"

The betel-nut chewer talked fast and excitedly. "All of the people high on the ridge where I live have heard that these women eat the muscle in the calves of the legs of all who listen to their teaching, then afterward inject water to make the leg look like everybody else's leg but without strength for walking or working. That's odd. I'm going back and I'll tell my people that you've got real muscles in your legs just like we have." He shuffled across the floor back to his own group where they all sat whispering and talking softly to each other.

The quietness afforded Dode and me a chance again to hear the conversation going on between Panot and Kardo. "Where do these women get the words they teach?" Kardo inquired of Panot. Panot leaned backward as far as he could without falling over completely and reached for our Bible lying on the floor beside some of the Bible pictures. He picked it up and showed it to Kardo. "Here's the source of all their teaching," he explained. "This is all Our Father's teaching, every page." Kardo reached across the fireplace and felt the paper. "These women," Panot went on, "don't do anything else except just sit and read this book all day, hunting for things to teach us." Now Dode's and my eyes got big. We gasped, but didn't dare contradict audibly.

Nothing else? We mentally defended ourselves—what about all the cleaning, laundering, cooking, carpentry, plumbing, cutting stencils, mimeographing lessons, writing Tadyawan songs, preparing reading primers and doctrine booklets, not to mention the hiking and the doctoring and the counselling? We raised our eyebrows and smiled across the floor to each other. We had no complaints. We thrived in our well-rounded missionary career. What did it really matter if they thought we didn't do anything!

Kardo seemed satisfied with Panot's explanation. "Yes," he remarked, "their teaching must be good teaching, for after they left last time, the widow here who sees the demons saw instead bright and beautiful children playing on our rooftop. It must have been those angels you talked about."

On subsequent visits Kardo reported other strange phenomena—bright lights outside the house for three nights following one of our visits, and a dream which told him he should listen to our teaching. One of his pagan people testified that when we walked up the path, he never saw demons following us but instead bright and shining beings at our heels. It was convincing evidence to Kardo and his household and would have produced a lasting interest in the Word of God had it not been for ill rumours that apprehensive tribesmen spread in the area. They claimed they had heard that we were actually demons posing as wonderful people. Others declared that we ate human beings, and they were frightened at being stewed alive in an imaginary huge cauldron that they had reportedly seen us carrying. Still others insisted that we had power to kidnap their men and hide them in big sacks and mail them off to our country for our cousins to eat. Each time Kardo relayed one of their fears to us, we reasoned with him from God's Word, and each time he accepted our explanations. Then pressure was put on Kardo by some of his more apprehensive subjects, and as his apparent interest in the Word grew, their fear and open opposition to it also grew.

"It's hard for us to believe here in my immediate household when the rest of my people don't want to come here to listen to the teaching," he said one day. "They say that if I follow your teaching, they will no longer follow me." Unlike most areas where leaders held undisputed sway and exercised full authority over their people, Kardo had competition from other powerful men with familiar spirits who vied for control. He couldn't afford to lose his prestige and power over so large an area. On succeeding visits we sensed a coldness and a purposeful disinterest, and nothing we said helped to warm the atmosphere. Discouragement set in in our own hearts, and each visit to Kardo's area became more painful. Kardo and his people absented themselves from the house when we were there, and gathering that this was the most gracious way they knew to tell us that we weren't really wanted, we visited less and less frequently.

One of our visits to Kardo's was very significant, however; not to Kardo, though, but instead to Bisi, our cooling Christian. Just prior to one of our visits, Mabilis, who had taken Panot's place as evangelist, came down with a bad cold and since tribal culture forbade a man to enter any home when he had a cold, Mabilis knew he would not be received at Kardo's. "What shall I do about it?" he asked just as we were leaving to trek back to town to get some prayer letters written and into the mail before going on to Kardo's.

"You're supposed to meet us in town three days from now," we said, "so if your cold isn't any better, ask one of the other men to take your place."

Three days later, when we answered the knock on our door in town, there standing beside Kalobang was Bisi. Our hearts sank, but we guarded our reactions, wondering privately all the time why Mabilis had asked Bisi to substitute for him when Bisi was still obviously out of touch with the Lord, being disgruntled, uncooperative, and generally ugly in disposition. He would have been the last person we would have chosen to go on the trip, but because he came we could only accept the fact that the Lord makes no mistakes and that maybe even his coming was for a very definite purpose. We only later learned that it was the gracious hand of the Lord that had moved Mabilis to ask Bisi to go. During the visit Bisi helped a lot with the teaching, urging Kardo's people to leave their sin and to follow the Lord. We were encouraged to think that maybe things would change for Bisi and he would return to the Lord himself. But once more back at the Bansod, after a disheartening and unresponsive visit, Bisi evaded us as much as before and only occasionally came to the Bible studies.

Months passed. The situation at Kardo's hadn't improved at all, but progress was made in the Bansod River area. Samuel was walking without holding on. Lutero and Dalioman had been sent by the church to Bible school and were almost at the end of their first year, and the other believers were growing in their practical understanding of the Word of God.

By this time Dode had gone on furlough and Hanni Kaspar, a capable nurse from Switzerland, along with Jean Govan, our Irish lass, were now permanent members of the team. We three had been in town for a few days when some of the Tadyawan dropped by, having come to town to sell their prepared rattan. While Hanni put on a big pot of rice and Jean cut up some fresh vegetables for their lunch, I helped them divide up the money they had earned from selling the rattan. When their financial matters were settled and aromas from the kitchen suggested that lunchtime was near, one of them pushed into my hand a crinkled note, folded up to about one inch square. I recognized Bisi's writing and opened it, thinking he was asking us to buy him a can of sardines or some batteries for his flashlight while we were in town. I was not prepared for the shocking content of the note, but there it lay in my hand, giving the explanation of the whole ugly problem of the past year or so. Bisi wrote: "What I am going to say isn't good. It's sorrowful. We have departed from God's path. We have sinned, that is, my niece Dorcas and I. We have fallen into the mire. But I want to return to God. Tell me how. I know the blood of Jesus washes us clean."

My heart rejected the implications of the note. Surely he didn't mean that, I reasoned with myself. Surely it's something else—maybe something connected with the pig that mysteriously wandered about unhindered in our village without anybody explaining its presence. Someone had slipped in conversation once, calling it a stolen pig. Surely that's what it must be. Maybe they had a part in that.

The note hastened our return to the hills for a private talk with Bisi. My first short, agonizing interview with him confirmed my gravest fears. He *had* committed adultery with his niece, Dorcas. While I appreciated his note of confession and his affirmation that he had stopped sinning in this way, still I was worried, for neither his tone nor his manner during our interview showed any sign of brokenness but rather a proud and arrogant spirit. Bisi had been a prominent leader in the church, quick to understand the principles of God, authoritative, yet understanding and capable of giving good, practical advice. The Tadyawan had respected his opinions and often followed his suggestions. But those days had now faded, for he had forfeited his honour, and he knew it. But from what I could gather in our interview, the experience hadn't humbled him but instead hardened him. He claimed that everybody in the church knew about his sin, for he had done it openly.

When I interviewed Dorcas, she too admitted their sin and confirmed the fact that they had stopped their sinning. "How long has it been since you stopped?" I asked.

"He sent me a note," she answered with head hanging down, "just after he returned from the evangelistic trip to Kardo's place. He said he knew we were wrong, and we would have to stop." I was amazed. We would never have thought of suggesting Bisi for that trip to Kardo's, but God *did* have a reason; he wanted to bring Bisi back to Himself and to us all!

Because Bisi was a church leader and Dorcas a faithful helper, the problem belonged to the church. We approached them with misgivings, wondering if they would accept their responsibility for disciplining a sinning brother according to the Word of God. It would be their first time. They had studied about it, but they had never had to handle the problem themselves. We knew it wouldn't be easy for them, for they were all tightly bound together and protective of each other with a practised duplicity that only a demon culture can perfect. But to our amazement and great relief, the church agreed that it was right for the two guilty ones to be disciplined.

In my interview with Bisi, he had insisted that Dorcas should be sent back to her parents so that he wouldn't be faced with temptation day after day. When I expressed his view to the men of the church who had gathered to talk over the situation, they disapproved. "We can't do that," contradicted Mabilis, without wasting a second. "It wouldn't be right. Bisi knows Dorcas's parents aren't Christians and want her to marry a heathen man. That's why she came up here to our village to live in the first place. To send her back would keep Bisi from sinning again, that's true, but we've got to think of Dorcas. To me, it doesn't sound as if Bisi has repented yet, for when a man is genuinely repentant, he determines that he will not indulge in evil again whether the temptation is still there or not. It's always been that way; that's the teaching of our grandfathers."

Everybody agreed with Mabilis. There could be no compliance with Bisi's wishes. Dorcas was to remain. Once having decided that point, they talked over other measures, concluding that both must make public confession to the church and public declaration of future abstinence; they must attend all meetings, but not take part in public ministry or the Lord's Supper until they were restored to fellowship again. Dorcas must never go to the fields or roam the forest alone but must always be in the company of some older woman. Bisi must never go out to town without his wife if Dorcas was in the crowd.

All of us dreaded the arrival of the Sunday for the confessions. Dorcas spoke first, hardly audible, admitting to the sin and promising that she would not return to it. Bisi was much bolder, speaking in loud, more confident tones, saying that they had sinned, but that they didn't intend to do it any more. It was his promise to Our Father. Then Panot announced the church's discipline and dismissed the meeting with the promise to Bisi and Dorcas that from then on the subject was closed and no one would mention it again. We all went to our homes satisfied that the meeting went as well and as smoothly as it did.

But, unbeknown to us, Bisi was not satisfied. From one of the houses up on the hill behind the church we heard loud shouting and talking, but we paid no particular attention to it, thinking that many had gathered for the usual leisurely Sunday chat over hot roasted sweet potatoes. But later in the afternoon Pedro, arriving a little early for the afternoon service, stopped in to see us. He was all upset. "Did you hear it?" he asked us. "Bisi is very angry. We're worried about him. He's been shouting and ranting all afternoon, claiming that he's mad because the church didn't send Dorcas back to her parents like he had wanted. He says now that the church didn't do that, he's not going to do what he promised; he's going to continue sinning with Dorcas." We were stunned. "Bisi said," Pedro continued, "that he's only doing what a lot of people in the Bible did anyway; some of them had lots of wives, so what was wrong if he had two?"

The men gathered again that afternoon, more deeply concerned over this rebellious outburst. Bisi sent a note down to the church while they were meeting, the note reiterating all his afternoon threats.

"Oh," said Panot, troubled, "he is really hard. Our Father has told us some of the things that men did long ago, even though they believed in Him, but He tells us both sides—the ones who did wrong and the ones who did right, so that we'll decide to follow those who did the right. Our Father always gives us a choice. I guess Bisi hasn't seen that. No, our discipline is still right. We cannot change it to suit his wishes." And in that position all the men stood firm.

"Since he wrote to us, we should write him an answer," suggested Mabilis, and they did: "Bisi, the discipline we impose on you is for your good and for Dorcas's good. Your submitting to our discipline is your proof that you are sorry for your sin. If you refuse the church discipline, there is nothing more that we can do. We will just have to hand you over to Our Father for His discipline.''

We liked the sound of the note, but Mabilis squirmed a bit as if he wasn't entirely satisfied with it. "We should add one more sentence," he said. "Let's ask him, 'Aren't you afraid of God?'" Then he turned to everybody and added, "If he isn't afraid of God, there's nothing left for us to do. We could never win him back to our family fellowship again." There was unanimous approval of his suggestion. The sentence was added, and the letter was sent up the hill.

Since it was already getting dark when the note was sent, we didn't expect an answer that evening, but many were the prayers of the Christians in their homes that night, beseeching God for our prodigal. Bright and early in the morning when Hanni was still stirring the oatmeal over the fireplace, Bisi's wife came to our door with a little note. "My husband has had a miserable night," she said uneasily. "He couldn't sleep. He wants the church to have this right away."

I was afraid to open it, yet rushed to do so. Relief settled from head to toe as I read these words: "Thanks to the church at the Bansod. I will accept their discipline." After the Monday morning service, we all read the note again and rejoiced that Bisi, though not afraid of his church's discipline, was afraid of God's.

"But now, we've got to write him another note," suggested Mabilis, "so that there'll be no mistake about what his discipline is." And so they wrote, "We're glad to hear your words, and now we expect you to follow our measures. You will attend all meetings, but you will not take part in any public ministry. You will never go out without your wife if Dorcas is in the crowd. You will not eat Our Jesus' Supper until you have been restored. And now pray every day that you will not be tempted by the devil to do this thing again. We will pray for you too, and we will never talk about this matter again." And with that the matter was closed, except that we privately prayed that God would mellow our Jacob and make him an Israel.

God answered that prayer, and though in the following months there were still strong temptations to be rebellious, and a few defeats, Bisi showed deeper understanding and added patience in his dealings with fellow Christians. In time he became an active capable leader again. But then, quite suddenly he developed serious pneumonia and the Lord called him to serve where there were no temptations. Before he died, and knowing he was going to die, he called for some of his closest friends in the church and asked them, "Have you seen any sin in my life that maybe I haven't noticed. I want to have it all confessed and be clean before I go to see Our Father."

27 Enough of "Our Jesus" to Go Round

Things were happening all over Mindoro. In all six tribes churches were springing up—infant churches scattered all over the island and isolated from each other by mountains and rivers and endless forest. Because they needed each other for mutual growth, encouragement, and expansion, our missionaries, after much discussion with the tribal churches themselves, aided them in the formation of an inter-tribal fellowship. Each church sent two representatives to the planning committee meetings, where they discussed church problems and solutions and laid plans for evangelism and annual inter-tribal conferences. The Tadyawan church on the Bansod elected Panot and Mabilis as their representatives, and these two young men willingly left families and field-work for several days at a time, several times each year, to go up north to attend the meetings, sharing their church's experiences and learning from the experience of others.

But if these two men were asked to make sacrifices for the Lord's sake, so also were their wives; and on one special occasion, Mabilis's bright little wife, Atla, took up her cross and followed the Lord in death to her own rights. A planning committee meeting had been called for immediately prior to the annual conference, and as the time drew near, it was quite obvious that Atla's time was also drawing near for the birth of their second child. We kept a troubled eye on Atla and wondered if Mabilis should stay home from the meetings up north and someone else be appointed in his place—though none was as well qualified as he—or if the Lord was asking for yet another sacrifice. Even though tribal culture kept pregnancies on the forbidden list for conversation, we mentioned it to Mabilis one day just a week before the scheduled meetings. "Mabilis, what about Atla? Does she feel that you should go to the meetings?"

With reddened face, Mabilis picked at the wart on his knee and muttered, "Yes, I think so."

"Isn't the time drawing near when she'll need you to deliver her baby?" we asked more pointedly. He merely nodded his head. "Well, then, what shall we do?" we persisted. "If both you and Atla feel that you should go to the meetings, should we make arrangements for someone else to be on hand to deliver her baby if it should arrive before you get back, like, say, her uncle Manindok?"

Still looking as if he wished we hadn't raised the subject, he quietly said, "I'll ask her." Later that day he casually strode over to where we were hanging up our laundry and mentioned that what we had been talking about earlier was all settled. He had spoken to Manindok too, and Manindok had accepted the responsibility. We knew he would. Though not especially gifted along any line, he was always willing for whatever the Lord asked of him.

The following Sunday, however, just three days before Panot and Mabilis were to leave for the meetings, Manindok suddenly became ill, but because that particular Sunday was an extra busy day for us we hardly took note. Dode had returned from furlough just two weeks previously and was trying to get caught up on all the church's present needs and problems. My furlough was just three days away, and I was tying all my own ends together. Jean was giving last-minute instructions to the Sunday school teachers who would function on their own while we were all out to town; and Hanni dispensed medicine at our kitchen door, favourite gathering place for sufferers from headaches, fevers, ringworm, or ulcers, all wanting pills or ointments and a little loving attention. In the midst of all that, and while I was still going over my notes for the morning sermon, someone brought word that Dorcas was not following the disciplinary measures of the church; so we had to alert the newly elected elders of the church—Mabilis, Mapol and Marcos—to arrange to stay behind following the afternoon service for an elders' meeting. Little wonder that the significance of Manindok's illness escaped us.

Notwithstanding, one person was secretly alarmed—Atla. Fortunately, as I hurried across the clearing to ring the bell for church, I ran into Atla, carrying on her shoulders her little girlie, who at that moment was crying as if her heart would break.

"Hey, what's the matter with your little daughter?" I called in the most comforting and cheerful tones I could manage as I extricated myself from a mind cluttered with church and furlough details.

A worried Atla looked up at me, face open and imploring. She hesitated, looked down at her feet, then up again, managing a weak smile. Above the cries of her daughter, her words tumbled out, "My little girlie says, 'Don't let our daddy go now!'" I was surprised and disappointed. Did Atla feel that she couldn't do without Mabilis after all? Was she changing her mind about the sacrifice she had been willing to make earlier that week? In a way, I couldn't blame her. What other tribal woman would have consented to a man other than her husband delivering her baby? None, I knew. Yet, because no one seemed qualified enough to take Mabilis's place at the planning committee, I felt the Lord was asking this sacrifice of Atla. She had always followed her husband faithfully in the things of the Lord, but now the Lord was asking for something that would cost her personally, to prove her love to Him. I stood there looking into her big dark eyes, so near to tears themselves. I hardly knew what to say. Should I challenge her to go all the way to Calvary, or should I be sympathetically practical? I never for one moment thought of Manindok stretched out on the floor of his house groaning with fever. But in the silence of those seconds, as I watched her, the thought was pushed forcefully into my mind—Manindok! Of course! That's what she is worried about. Manindok is sick, and now Atla isn't sure whether or not she can count on his help.

"Oh, Atla," I said with a sigh of relief. "It's because Manindok is sick, isn't it? That's why you're worried." Grateful eyes and a big smile said all the "yes" I needed. "What about your brother, Mapol? Would you be satisfied to have him perform the delivery if need be?" I suggested.

"Yes, that would be fine," she answered, "but he lives so far away—three whole rice-cookings walking time from here. He lives in this village only at the weekends; suppose . . ."

"Shall we ask him if he could help?" I interrupted.

"Yes, but I'd like you to ask him," and with that she smiled shyly, reminding me that I was discussing a forbidden topic.

I hastened over to Mapol's weekend house. "Why sure," he agreed grinning broadly. "Mabilis'll be gone for only a week. Our Father will help me with my field-work afterward. My family and I will just stay right here in case Atla needs me."

Atla gave me one of her best smiles when I passed the word on to her a few minutes later.

That Wednesday dawned bright and clear. It was the day for Panot and Mabilis to leave for the north. Mabilis packed his belongings into his sack and called after Panot who had preceded him on to the trail, "Wait for me at the river."

"Sure," echoed back Panot's voice. Mabilis turned and said goodbye to his family, and then crouching through the doorway, sprang to the ground, and headed down the trail, leaving behind him his happy wife, his little girlie, and his newborn son. Our Father, surely pleased with the sacrifices His children were learning to make, sent the baby along the day before its daddy had to leave.

When the men came back from the committee meetings and conference, I had already left for furlough, and therefore missed first-hand the enthusiasm and fresh joy that was theirs; but letters from Dode, Jean, and Hanni gave me all the details. The men had been so encouraged and challenged to continue plodding on in evangelism that they vigorously sought to stir up the rest of the church. The church needed the encouragement, for in their efforts to spread the gospel they were encountering impregnable defiance. Pidyong's area was still closed to the gospel, as was Tigaw, the area where Kalobang's cousin lived; and Kardo's group, while never prohibiting visits, showed continuing fear and suspicion and a resulting lack of interest in the Word of God. Other Tadyawan in scattered areas developed only short-lived concern, being turned quickly away either by false rumours or threats from their leaders. And Bilbino—the one who, through long years of storm and despair had held with unbelievable tenacity to the hope offered by the early vision—had never surrendered to the message of the Good News when it came. Though most of his sons and daughters and in-laws became Christians, he stubbornly chose to sit in the shadows of unbelief, continuing to communicate with his wise-one and aggressively opposing the gospel, seeking to dissuade those of his own village and those who visited them. With no encouragement other than the Lord's "Go ye" the Tadyawan church needed that faith for evangelism that would "not shrink, though pressed by every foe."

One Sunday several months before I left for furlough, Mabilis was sitting on the church floor, with us and all the believers sitting side by side in a circle around him as he led us in the observance of the Lord's Supper. The elements, a roasted sweet potato and cups of red sugar-cane juice, were in front of him. He reached out and pulled toward him the enamel plate with the potato on it. Then taking the potato in his hand, he began slowly to break it in pieces. As he broke it, he said, "When Our Jesus fed His disciples on that last night before He died, He first broke the bread so that there would be enough to go round. That's His illustration and picture to us. His body was broken too, like the bread, for us all. There's enough of Our Jesus to go round—enough for everybody who wants Him. That's why we must go and teach others, even if it's hard."

My heart still says "Amen". Is it not the Lord Himself who works with them, the One who "frustrates the omens of the liars, and makes fools of diviners; who turns wise men back, and makes their knowledge foolish; who confirms the word of his servant and performs the counsel of his messengers"?[1] Surely as there was God's "fullness of time" for the Bansod group, there will be a "fullness of time" for the untangling of other Tadyawan from the snare of the devil and establishing of additional Tadyawan churches on the island of Mindoro.

[1] Isaiah 45.25 ASV.

Publisher's Note

The continuing story of the Mangyan Church will have to be told one day. Already an Association of Churches binds the Christians in all six tribes together; an inter-tribal Church conference draws hundreds each dry season; the Mangyan Bible School trains chosen representatives for the leadership of the churches; and an inter-tribal teachers' training school is providing primary school teachers for the forest schools. Christian Filipino lawyers are doing all they can to secure justice for the Mangyan, title deeds to the land they have occupied and tilled for generations, and protection from the unscrupulous men and exploitation to which they have been victims for so long.

Over on the western side of the island many more Mangyan wait for the gospel to be taken to them. Mangyan missionaries of each tribe are searching out their fellow-tribesmen in the deepest recesses of the island. In Mindanao, after Luzon the largest island in the Philippines chain, more forest tribes await the gospel. In some the Wycliffe Bible Translators have been mastering the languages and translating Scripture, but evangelists, church-planters, are needed to build on these foundations. Experienced missionaries from Mindoro are to pioneer this venture, but here also new blood is needed, young reinforcements willing to endure hardship for Christ's sake.

Note: The tribal people of Mindoro, in all six tribes, are collectively known as "Mangyan".